Exploring Quality Practice in Key Stage 1

Continuous Provision is an effective vehicle for reflecting young children's interests, supporting learning in a developmentally appropriate way and for implementing and embedding the curriculum. However, whilst its value is consistently recognised across Early Years settings, what it means to Key Stage 1 practitioners, and what it looks like in practice varies greatly, and its impact on learning and outcomes for children is similarly wide-ranging.

At Early Excellence, we believe that the effective use of high-quality continuous provision alongside well-planned enhanced provision and adult-led, directed activities, continues to be a highly effective approach to teaching and learning, leading to impactful and sustained outcomes for 5-7 year olds.

This guide seeks to provide you with a clear understanding of the principles that underpin this approach, as well as being a practical tool to support you in planning and evaluating provision.

We hope that you and your colleagues find it really useful.

Liz Marsden.

Liz Marsden, CEO and all the
Team at Early Excellence

Continuing with Provision in Key Stage 1 The Reasons Why

Providing rich opportunities to apply learning in context

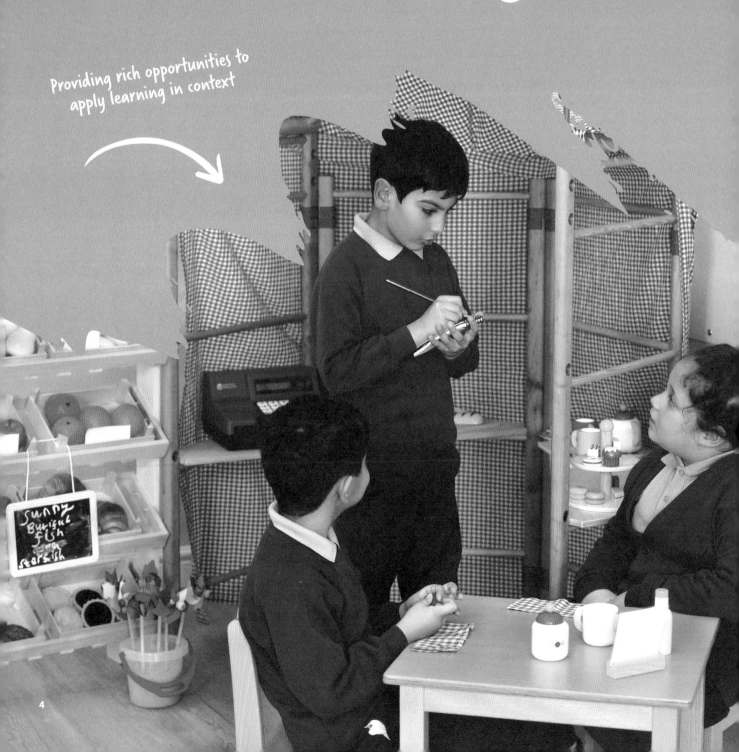

When we think about the place of continuous provision in our primary schools, we often think of our youngest children only. Most 3-, 4- and 5-year olds are able to learn in an exciting, dynamic environment with opportunities for child-led learning, inside and out.

In a good EYFS setting, children's interests and developmental needs are at its heart. It offers a carefully planned, well-resourced learning environment supported by adults who understand how to engage with, guide and extend young children's thinking through skilful interaction.

There is a clear understanding in the EYFS that children need to experience their learning first-hand in order to explore and make sense of the world, and that this exploration supports the development of critical learning behaviours.

By the end of their reception year, most children have developed far greater confidence, are more creative and highly independent.

Unfortunately, in quite a lot of schools, as children move into Key Stage 1 the time to explore freely and learn through self-initiated activities is significantly reduced, and at worst reserved only for playtimes. This goes against everything that we understand about child development and the fact that key developmental changes in how children learn do not usually occur until around the age of 7.

Why then, only six weeks after leaving Reception, might children enter a space and an environment for learning that is entirely different from the one they left; where the autonomy they previously enjoyed has all but disappeared?

Often, the move to National Curriculum expectations and the pressure of 'coverage', as well as the requirement for evidence in books in order to demonstrate progress, precipitates a significant increase in whole class teaching sessions following prescribed content and approaches. This often requires a rigid timetable leaving little time, if any, for applying learning in context, for problem solving, creative and critical thinking.

This can lead to approaches where the more practical elements of teaching and learning, including opportunities for child-initiated learning, are squeezed in or added as a time filler for children finding it difficult to access the core curriculum. As Julie Fisher* suggests, when adults see play as merely recreational or a waste of learning time, its considerable value is overlooked.

* The Importance of Play in Key Stage 1, Julie Fisher Foundation Stage Forum (2020)

So, why should we continue to facilitate child-led learning throughout Key Stage 1?

1. Well-being

First and foremost, when children are in a stimulating environment and have time for spontaneous, child-led learning they not only find learning more enjoyable but are also more highly motivated.

Professor Dr. Ferre Laevers argues that when children are so closely connected to a situation and their involvement is high, then their well-being improves. He explains that well-being is not just reliant on positive, strong relationships, but is dependent on a sense of satisfaction and a belief in one's own competencies.

A UK study published by the Department for Education* found that pupil well-being can predict later academic progression and engagement in school. For example, pupils with better emotional well-being at age 7 had a value-added Key Stage 2 score, 2.46 points higher (equivalent to more than one term's progress) than pupils with poorer emotional wellbeing.

This sends a powerful message that continuing to offer an environment rich in opportunities for practical, self-initiated activities is vital throughout Key Stage 1.

2. Life-long Learning Skills

In addition, child-led learning challenges children to overcome problems in a wide range of meaningful contexts; problems that are social and emotional, as well as intellectual. As they do so, children develop confidence in their own abilities and the independent, creative and critical thinking that we know underpins successful, lifelong learners.

The Characteristics of Effective Learning (CoEL) which have been at the heart of the EYFS since 2012 and form a vital part of planning and observing in the EYFS, are relevant at any age or stage. These characteristics, sometimes referred to as learning behaviours or dispositions, can create a valuable framework for reflecting on effective teaching and learning throughout the school; some primary schools already take this approach, with great success.

The powerful potential of provision to support children's learning behaviours

Playing & Exploring – Engagement
Finding out and exploring
Playing with what they know
Being willing to 'have a go'

Active Learning – Motivation
Being involved and concentrating
Keeping trying
Enjoying achieving what they set out to do

Creating and Thinking Critically – Thinking
Having their own ideas
Making links
Choosing ways to do things

Whilst the content of the teaching will change and move on from the EYFS, as will our expectations of the children - the effectiveness of the learning process is paramount and the CoEL provide a very useful common language.

3. Making Links, Embedding Skills & Knowledge

In 'Why Ages 2-7 Matter So Much for Brain Development', Sriram* writes that the period of brain development between the ages of 2 and around 7 offers 'a prime opportunity to lay the foundation for a holistic education for children'

Here, he explains that there are four ways to maximise this period by:
- Encouraging a love of learning
- Focusing on breadth instead of depth
- Paying attention to emotional intelligence
- Not treating young children's education as merely a precursor to "real" learning

More recently, research undertaken by the Education Endowment Foundation* reveals growing evidence of the powerful relationship between self-regulation and metacognition. This reminds us of the critical need to provide opportunities for children to 'Plan, Monitor and Evaluate their own activities; to draw on their prior experiences, set their own challenges and connect learning across the curriculum; driven by self-motivation.'

Encouraging a life-long love of learning

* DFE Study England
(2014)

* Why Ages 2-7 Matter So Much for Brain Development, Sriram (2020)

* Metacognition and Self-Regulated Learning, Quigley, Muijs & Stringer Education Endowment Foundation (2018)

What does this imply for Key Stage 1?

It tells us that crucially, when time often feels limited, opportunites for child-led learning in an effective Key Stage 1 environment do not take children away from learning, but rather support it.

When you observe children working efficiently in provision, you see the curriculum in action, links are made, and skills and knowledge revisited.

As children engage with provision, as they manipulate tools and resources and explore their ideas, key concepts come to life in meaningful contexts that help embed knowledge and deepen understanding.

As Julie Fisher writes, child-initiated learning is '.. unpredictable, but few of its surprises lie outside the skills and concepts we will want Year 1 and Year 2 children to learn. The learning that emerges is often of a very high order. Once the teacher is competent at evaluating it, play provides a rich source of information for planning the rest of the curriculum.'*

This means that when children have the support of adults who are skilled in observing and identifying learning, who can recognise the gaps in skills and knowledge, and pinpoint what is needed next – then their learning will flourish.

Child-led learning is not, of course, enough on its own to ensure progress, nor does it supplant the adult in the classroom: skills and knowledge need to be thoroughly planned and effectively taught. But done well, embracing child-led learning brings the joy of discovery and achievement, gives a place where children's interests are truly valued, and individual strengths recognised and celebrated.

* Moving On to Key Stage 1,
Julie Fisher
Open University Press
(2020)

Activity 1
Evaluating Your Vision

As a team, work together to discuss where you are now, in relation to child-led learning, and where you would like to be:

– How do you structure the learning environment? What does your classroom layout look like? Are there areas for independent, child-led learning?

– What resources and materials are available for children to access independently? How are these introduced/modelled?

– How much emphasis is placed on the well-being of the child?

– How far does the development of children's learning behaviours and dispositions (CoEL) impact on your approach to teaching and learning?

Valuing children's interests and individual strengths

Think

Plan

Do

Review

What do we mean by Continuous Provision in Key Stage 1 ?

Supporting and extending children's learning with carefully resourced provision areas

"To me, education is about developing certain dispositions in children. These dispositions should include being reflective, inquisitive, inventive, resourceful, full of wonder (wonder – full?), wonderment and puzzlement. These dispositions should include the habits of searching for evidence; they also include the dispositions to be tender, courageous, caring, compassionate and should certainly include some humour as well".

Last Class Notes, 2007
Lilian G. Katz

In this section we consider how to develop an approach in Key Stage 1 that builds on the EYFS and continues to provide opportunities for independent learning of sufficient challenge.

In order for this pedagogical approach to be established, we need to develop a highly effective, well-planned learning environment that offers three distinct, yet complementary strands of learning and teaching.

To help us, let's first consider the Early Excellence Curriculum Model shown on this page. This model for Key Stage 1, mirrors much of the EYFS model but adds greater emphasis on directed activities with a larger proportion of the whole class and small group instruction.

In the model you can see how Continuous Provision, in tandem with Enhanced Provision, acts as the foundation for meaningful experiences that underpin and give context to the curriculum.

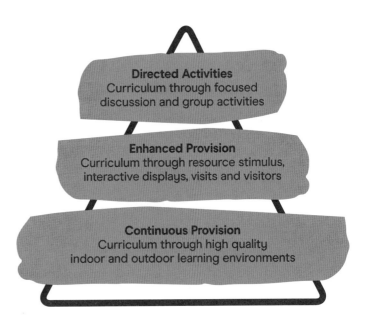

Directed Activities
Curriculum through focused discussion and group activities

Enhanced Provision
Curriculum through resource stimulus, interactive displays, visits and visitors

Continuous Provision
Curriculum through high quality indoor and outdoor learning environments

In a well-resourced environment that offers an appropriate blend of provision, there will be countless opportunities for children to pursue their innate curiosity, follow their interests as well as revisit, practice and embed the skills and knowledge we teach them; all of which ensures a high degree of challenge and nurtures deep-level learning.

You will also see a strong focus on adult-led teaching and learning through Directed Activities. These include activities planned for carefully identified groups of children and whole class input, as part of the curriculum. During these activities, adults introduce the learning, provide instruction, model skills, demonstrate methods of working and give practical examples of how to solve problems.

As children move through Key Stage 1, not all directed activities will require an adult. Sometimes children will work on tasks alongside an adult, but they will also be asked to complete tasks with increasing independence. How long children can be expected to remain on task will need regular assessment. Many children can only complete adult directed activities independently for short periods of time before they lose concentration and/or seek help. Planning too many activities and expecting children to stick at these for too long, can lead to long queues by the teacher and much time wasting!

An alternative strategy is to plan only a few group activities, perhaps one adult working with one group or maybe two groups at once, to ensure that the learning takes place. Other children will be sufficiently engaged in their own investigations within provision (child-led or adult-introduced) supported, where possible, by an additional adult if available.

What is Continuous Provision?

As in the EYFS, we use the term Continuous Provision to describe the provision areas available to children on a daily basis. Each provision area contains a core set of resources that children are able to access and use independently, with the resources and the way they are organised remaining largely constant throughout the year. In this way, children are offered a familiar environment in which they can sustain their interests, practice new skills, make links between different areas of knowledge and develop their ideas over time.

Each provision area can be enriched throughout the year by extending the resources included or aspects of organisation, in line with the children's progress. In this way you might, for example, enhance a block area with images of buildings or other structures as well as maps and aerial photographs of different settings or landscapes; or add labelling that references repeated addition or multiplication statements based on the arrays used to organise the blocks, or the height and/or diameter of the blocks displayed.
To help you visualise what well organised provision in Key Stage 1 might look like, we have included a number of examples on pages 16-17.

What is Enhanced Provision?

Alongside the development of Continuous Provision, we promote the use of enhancements as a way of extending children's learning and responding to their interests. These additions do not replace any of the core Continuous Provision resources, rather they are added to provide a new dimension to what is already there for a finite period of time.

Enhancements can be effectively used in order to:
– Recognise and respond to children's current interests or fascinations
– Reflect and extend children's current learning
– Introduce experiences and resources related to future learning

They include resources, materials and equipment, visits and visitors and will need adult support to introduce them and guide children's explorations.

For example: small world figures relating to a current text or theme; natural resources reflecting the seasons; the equipment required to construct an electrical circuit; or a visit to a nearby site of interest; a supermarket, sports centre or historical building; these can all be used to add to capitalise on children's curiosity and enrich the learning experience.

Enhancements do not need to be added to every area and are not needed all the time. It is important to judge how many you need to have at any one time, based on what will be of most value to your children and how you can manage these alongside the learning taking place in continuous provision and your group work.

Highly accessible carefully presented resources to stimulate engagement

How to Arrange & Organise Provision in Key Stage 1

When planning a Key Stage 1 classroom, it is best to begin by reviewing all of the space available. Consider not only the classroom/s but any adjoining or shared spaces that may be able to be developed. Space is often at a premium in Key Stage 1 and this can be one of the biggest barriers to development, so you will need to be creative when planning which elements of provision you wish to include.

Continuous Provision is best organised by using furniture to divide the available space into smaller areas or bays. In each of these distinct areas, a selection of resources will be chosen. For each area the resources are carefully selected and presented in a way that is both appealing and accessible to children, and which maximises learning opportunities.

In this example of a Key Stage 1 classroom, you can see how the furniture has been planned to create defined areas around the room, including in the middle of the space. Provision is not confined to the edges of the room and tables for the children form part of some areas with focus tables also available.

How to Prioritise Areas of Continuous Provision

The space available will dictate some of the decisions made regarding which areas to include. In a small classroom not all areas are possible, so it is best to prioritise according to the needs of the children, your curriculum and what will work best for the cohort and classroom.

Some areas can be combined such as art and design, and some experiences can be offered in different ways, through taught sessions, for example. Whatever choices you and your team make as you plan your classrooms, make sure to establish a breadth of curriculum coverage through your provision.

Selecting Your Areas

Carpet / Dry Floor Surface

Maths Area
A key area of provision including resources for number work as well as for exploring shape, space and measure. Include a table and chairs.

Blocks & Small World Area
Two areas that work best when sharing a large floor space protected from through-traffic.

Construction Area
An area for two or three construction kits with additional open-ended resources. Works best when separated from blocks. Could be best organised where the whole class gather.

Writing Area
A key area of provision that includes tables, chairs and access to a range of drawing and writing materials.

Books & Puppets Area
Fiction texts including poetry, sometimes with puppets. A quiet, welcoming space with cushions/comfortable seating.

Role Play Area
If you have the space, include a themed or an open-ended role play area. Include storage for core resources, an open space that can be developed into a range of settings. A frame structure with small table and chairs will support this.

Enquiry Area
A key area for non-fiction texts with a focus on research and investigation of your current topic, as well as for children's own interests. Needs shelving, table and chairs.

Messy / Wet Flooring, if available

Sand Area
An area that can be developed in miniature if you lack space for a large sand tray. Would also work in a sheltered outdoor space.

Water Area
Another area that can be in miniature using bowls. Would also work in a sheltered outdoor space.

Art Area
If possible, provide separate painting and drawing areas, but these can be combined.

Workshop Area
A large space, if possible, to support craft, DT and box modelling. Works well if children can stand, rather than sit at tables. Place close to the art area.

Activity 2
Developing Your Provision

As a team, work together to discuss which areas of provision to prioritise, based on the space available and the needs of your children. If possible, use information about your cohort to help you plan provision and experiences.

- What are the needs of your children?

- What are their prior experiences?

- What are your main priorities for learning in your curriculum?

- What are the most important areas of provision that you and your team need to review and develop?

Discussing cohort information to evaluate and develop provision

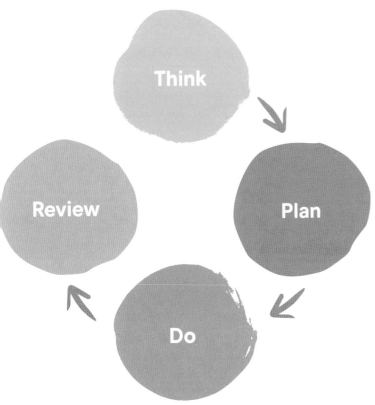

Think

Plan

Do

Review

Examples of Provision
in Key Stage 1

Small construction sets presented in a range of transparent boxes with a display table alongside

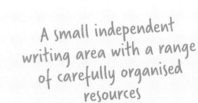

A small independent writing area with a range of carefully organised resources

A well equipped maths area displaying resources to support number, space, shape & measure

A range of artefacts and books displayed attractively in an enquiry area

A themed role-play area offering real-life opportunities for applying key learning

The Impact of Continuous Provision

Developing children's dispositions, their confidence and independence

Thinking about the Child

The Development Model begins with 'The Child' and what we know about the nature of early childhood. As highlighted in Section 1, Birth-7yrs is a very particular period of development. Children in Key Stage 1 are growing rapidly, they are exploring and making sense of the world, developing relationships and learning how to identify and manage their feelings and behaviour. Children of 5, 6 and 7 continue to need the security of a trusted adult, clear boundaries and an achievable level of challenge in order to thrive.

The freedom that Continuous Provision provides for children to make their own choices, means that they are more likely to experience satisfaction, sustain motivation and persist when faced with a problem and therefore far more likely to view themselves as successful learners.

How does Continuous Provision support and deepen learning in Key Stage 1?

In this section, we start by introducing the Early Excellence Development Model for Key Stage 1 found below. This is a useful tool used to illustrate the inter-relationship between the child's learning needs, the environment and the role of the adult.

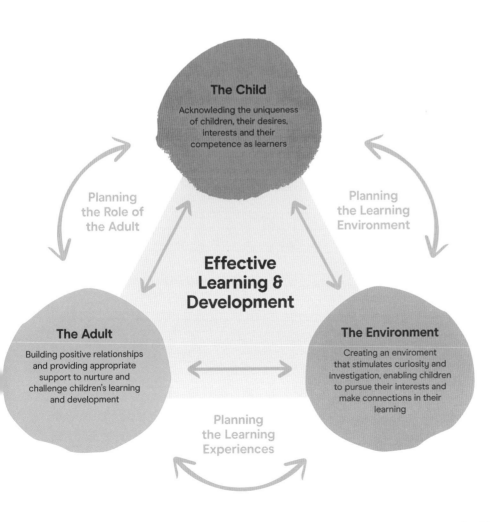

The Child
Acknowleding the uniqueness of children, their desires, interests and their competence as learners

Planning the Role of the Adult

Planning the Learning Environment

Effective Learning & Development

The Adult
Building positive relationships and providing appropriate support to nurture and challenge children's learning and development

The Environment
Creating an enviroment that stimulates curiosity and investigation, enabling children to pursue their interests and make connections in their learning

Planning the Learning Experiences

Thinking about the Environment

The next strand of our Development Model is 'The Environment', the setting which provides a context for children to explore their ideas and apply what they have been taught. A well-planned environment supports an active approach to learning that Key Stage 1 children require, and it provides the opportunity to revisit, practice and embed what they know or are being taught. This supports the mastery of key skills and concepts enabling children to consolidate their knowledge and build their understanding.

Once the space has been defined and provision areas created, offering consistency of resources and organisation is vital. Knowing what is available to them and where it is kept, supports independence and enables children to follow a train of thought without the frustration that can arise when a resource or tool they need is no longer available. This in turn means that children are far more likely to remain on task and follow their ideas through to a conclusion, rather than giving up or 'flitting' somewhat aimlessly between areas.

Thinking about the Adult

This third strand covers many aspects of the adult role including planning and timetabling, direct teaching sessions with groups and individuals as well as interacting and observing children engaged in self-initiated activities.

It cannot be stressed enough, just how much the role of the adult matters and how the rhythm of each day and the time available, is used to teach as much as possible. Teach, in its broadest definition, from welcoming children into the classroom at the start of the day, leading a whole class session, guiding small group work, through to more personal interactions to support child-led learning and manage daily issues and behaviours as they arise.

It is obvious to state that whole class instruction would be weak without an adult as in fact it couldn't exist without the adult! The same is true though of child-led learning. While it can exist, it will be weak and easily deteriorate in quality and impact without regular adult support and attention.

Offering opportunities for children to use continuous and enhanced provision will only be successful if adults devote time to support, enhance and extend the learning that is taking place.

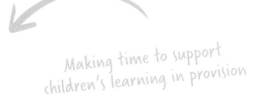

Making time to support children's learning in provision

Activity 3
Strengthen Your Provision

As a team, work together to discuss how effective each strand of the development model is currently, in your setting:

– How do the interests and motivations of your children impact on your planning in both the medium and short term?

– How well does your environment support children's independence? Are resources consistently available to them when they need them? Do they work with them effectively?

– Do the adults in your setting spend as much time planning, supporting and observing learning in provision as they do to learning that they lead?

Evaluating the effectiveness of each provision area

How to Plan Continuous Provision

Organising the effective use
of space and resources

To support you in developing your areas of provision, you will find a set of planning guides at the back of this booklet.

The guides outline all of the learning possibilities for each area of provision, structured to fit with the Key Stage 1 National Curriculum in England*. However, whichever curricular you use, the opportunities for learning will be very similar.

Alongside the National Curriculum links, the plans present you with a way to consider and document five key elements:

- The resources available for the children to use
- How best to organise your resources to maximise their learning potential
- What you intend to see the children doing in each area, the experiences offered
- The recording opportunities available in each area
- The learning behaviours that you expect children to exhibit when working in an area

We recommend that you study the 'How to' guide first with your team, before developing your own plans. Whilst we have included detailed plans for each area as a guide, it is important that your plans accurately reflect the unique nature of your provision, the needs of your cohort and curriculum.

By working with your team on creating your own set of plans, you will have the opportunity to develop a shared understanding of the rationale behind each provision area in order that you can all articulate the relationship between provision, children's learning and the curriculum. The level of consistency that will result from this is critical and will be of great benefit to your children.

Selecting Resources

The key thing to remember when deciding about which resources to include in each area, is that every resource needs to earn its place. It's important to identify what children will naturally want to do, to understand the specific needs of your children and know your curriculum, what you need to teach.

The resources you select for each area should enable children to explore their ideas and further embed a wide range of key skills, concepts and vocabulary – so careful planning is vital. You should also consult with Early Years colleagues to ensure that the resources are supporting progression.

* National Curriculum in England
Department for Education (2013)

Identifying which Areas of Continuous Provision to Prioritise

Space, and sometimes resources, are often at a premium in Year 1 and Year 2, so it may not be possible to include all the areas of provision referenced in this guide.

Do not feel that it is necessary to fit all of the provision areas in. It is far better to include a smaller number of areas with sufficient space and enough resources for your children to use effectively.

Decisions about which areas to include should be made based on the needs of your cohort but also, from a practical point of view, which you are able to resource.

The following tables are designed to aid you as you decide which areas of continuous provision to develop or rethink.

How many shall I buy? Opportunities to apply mathematical thinking in context

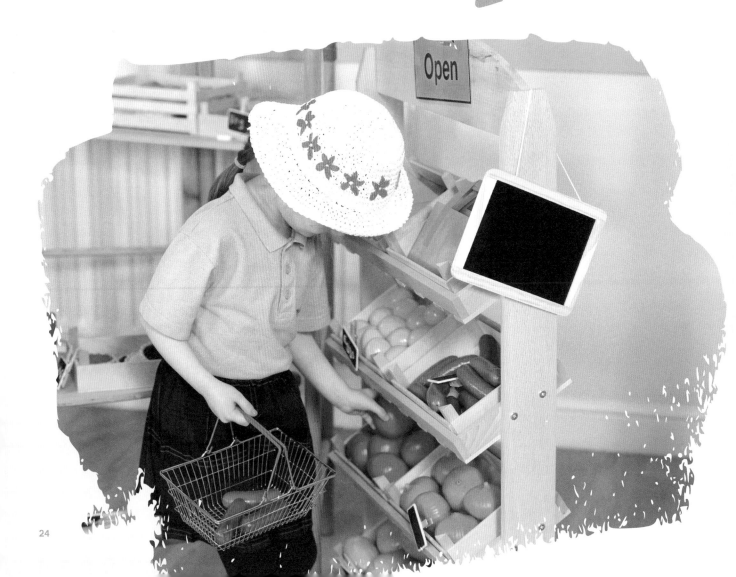

Areas Rich in Opportunities for Language and Literacy

Writing

- Developing confidence in writing
- Opportunities to refine handwriting, and reinforce phonic and grammatical knowledge
- Embedding taught skills

Small World

- Creating settings and characters
- Developing and recording narratives
- Writing signs, captions and labels

Role Play

- Playing and consolidating speech and language used in familiar and imaginative contexts

Books & Puppets

- Developing a love of books
- Opportunities to select from a range of books
- Understanding narrative structure
- Embedding reading skills

Enquiry

- Acquiring information from non-fiction texts
- Understanding the difference between fiction and non-fiction
- Extending vocabulary
- Writing notes and labelling diagrams

Sand & Water

- Creating story settings
- Developing real-life and imaginative narratives

Areas Rich in Opportunities for Maths

Maths

- Counting, recognising and understanding number
- Reinforcing an understanding of place value
- Playing games that reinforce aspects of mathematical learning
- Working with measurement for length, mass, capacity and time

Construction

- Experiencing the properties of shape
- Using measurement of length in context
- Drawing accurate representations of their models
- Using positional and comparative language to discuss their ideas and structures

Blocks

- Naming shapes and identifying their properties
- Using measurements and fractions in a meaningful context
- Positioning and sequencing blocks including opportunities for tessellation, reflection and rotation

Role Play

- Reading and writing numbers in context
- Opportunities to use time in meaningful contexts, including timetables and appointments
- Learning about money, and using coins with understanding

Sand & Water

- Exploring and using the language of capacity, making comparisons between amounts and containers
- Reading scales

Areas Rich in Opportunities for Science

Enquiry

- Asking questions and following lines of enquiry to find answers
- Working with a range of sources including reference texts and artefacts
- Observing carefully and commenting on what they see
- Using simple equipment to observe and test

Sand

- Investigating sand as a material
- Exploring movement, force, speed and direction
- Investigating, predicting, testing and solving problems
- Exploring materials and how their properties can be changed

Workshop

- Identifying and naming materials
- Selecting resources according to their properties

Water

- Investigating water as a material and how it moves
- Exploring movement, force, speed and direction

Areas Rich in Opportunities for Art and Design & Technology

Art

- Refining skills in working with a range of tools, techniques and media
- Using the approach of other artists and craftworkers to influence their own work
- Making decisions about the skills and materials that best suit their purpose
- Becoming confident in their ability as artists

Construction

- Planning and building from a design
- Adding details or props to their designs
- Exploring and using mechanisms
- Making links to real life examples

Role Play

- Creating props to support and enhance their role play settings and narratives

Workshop

- Using a range of techniques, tools and materials to enhance their models
- Generating and developing ideas
- Selecting from a range of materials and components to create mock-ups, models and structures
- Exploring and using mechanisms
- Investigating how structures can be made stronger and more stable

Blocks & Small World

- Recognising colour, texture, pattern, form and space as elements of building
- Creating imaginative scenery and props to enhance their settings and narratives
- Generating ideas through talking, drawing and mock-ups
- Making links to the work of artists and designers and to real world examples

Areas Rich in Opportunities for History, Geography and RE

Enquiry

- Using a range of sources including texts, artefacts and photographs to aid enquiry about different places and times
- Referencing and deepening their understanding of maps and globes

Role Play

- Working with props that enhance role play and providing an opportunity to explore different contexts or settings through play

Books & Puppets

- Reading and retelling stories that highlight lives in different places or times
- Becoming familiar with texts and characters that are diverse and inclusive

Blocks & Small World

- Using technical vocabulary to describe natural and built features
- Recording structures and settings through maps, aerial and plan photography
- Developing knowledge of historical places and buildings

Using artifacts and texts to support enquiry

Exploring tools and techniques in a meaningful context

Making Curriculum Links

When making decisions about which areas to include you may want to consider which work well together, alongside each other. These include:

- **Blocks & Small World:** The blocks are used to create the structures around which children will develop settings and narratives with the small world resources
- **Role Play & Workshop:** Children can create props that support the role play areas they develop
- **Art & Workshop:** Once they have made a model in the workshop, children may decide to decorate and add finer details
- **Maths & Small Construction:** Maths and Construction combine to create a focus on engineering

Once your plans are written and each area of provision is established, it will be essential to regularly review how well they support your children. You will need to take time to consider whether all areas are used appropriately and above all, whether children are effectively supported by confident adults who ensure that children's learning needs are met?

Supporting children to enquire, deepen their knowledge and make links

Activity 4
Evaluating Your Provision

As a team, discuss how well each area of provision works and meets the needs of your children:

- Which areas are least effective and will need you to focus on most closely?
- Which are the most important to get right, based on the current needs of your children?

Using the planning guides for the areas you have identified, discuss with your team:

The resources
- Are they age-appropriate, of good quality and effective in supporting learning?
- Have you included open-ended resources?
- Have you enough resources to support a small group of children?
- Do all adults know how to use the resources?

Organisation
- Are the resources well-organised?
- Does the organisation reflect learning, where appropriate?
- Does the organisation support the children to tidy and maintain the area?

Experiences offered
- Do your children use the area as described?
- Are adults supporting the development of key vocabulary?

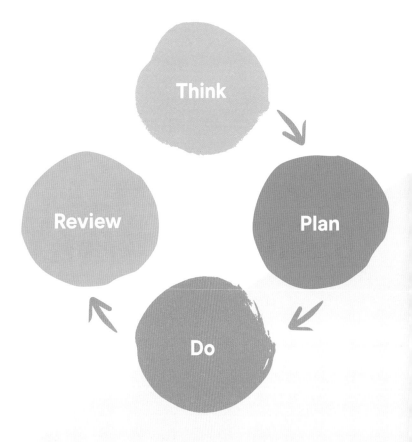

Developing the Adult Role

Can you see what is happening here? Exploring ideas and discussing theories

If using continuous and enhanced provision in Key Stage 1 alongside whole class and small group work is an approach you are developing in your school, then staff development will be crucial.

It's important to recognise just how skilful teachers need to be in Key Stage 1, being able to adopt different approaches at different times. In Key Stage 1 adults need to be facilitators of learning, problem solvers and guides to help move child-led learning forward, as well as instructors able to impart, explain and connect knowledge to ensure it has meaning for children.

This means that adults in Key Stage 1, much like those in Early Years, require a good understanding of how young children develop and learn and a thorough understanding of how to interact to maximise a wide range of learning situations, including whole class and small group, as well as child-led in all its many forms.

Adults also require an in-depth knowledge of National Curriculum expectations to ensure that all children make sufficient, ambitious progress. In this section we focus only on the role of the adult in continuous provision, remembering that child-led learning will only be successful if adults devote time to support and challenge children's thoughts and ideas as they are taking place.

Introducing Provision

To begin exploring the adult role in provision we look first at the importance of helping children to use each area, and each resource well.

The resources, expectations and opportunities that are available in Continuous Provision need careful introduction if they are to fully support child-led learning. It is well worthwhile devoting time to this, particularly at the beginning of the year and through the year when new or additional resources are added.

Think about whether children know what each resource is called and what it should and shouldn't be used for. In many cases, how to use the resources, tools and equipment will need to be taught directly, and opportunities planned to develop the skills required to work with them purposefully. This is vital ahead of children choosing to utilise them for their own purposes.

Take a paper fastener as an example. Do children know what it is called? How it is designed? How it can be safely used? Have they been shown how to use it in different contexts and been given opportunities for guided practice?

Setting High Expectations

What we intend children to learn as part of their self-initiated activity is heavily influenced by the expectations we set for our children's independence. We need to consider not only what the children will use but how they will access it, as well as how the resources and the area will be maintained.

In this example from Hemingford Grey Primary School, Cambridgeshire, staff have ensured that the paint is accessible to the children and that they have been taught how to select and mix the paint, as well as how to clear up afterwards. Responsibility for maintaining the area has been passed to the children, but with adult oversight at the end of every day.

A good way to pass responsibility to children is during 'Tidy up Time' when children in Year 1 and Year 2 can take more of a role in not only maintaining each area but also offering feedback and suggestions of what works well and how to make improvements.

For example, in the Book & Puppets Area children might be encouraged to suggest a book or an illustrator of the week and be responsible for making sure that these books are well displayed, or they may design simple ways to gather feedback about who has read the book of the week, or whether they liked it, and so on. One or two children might be given responsibility for introducing these ideas, books and proformas to the class and reporting back on responses.

Similarly, small groups may take responsibility for collecting, collating and presenting weather data.

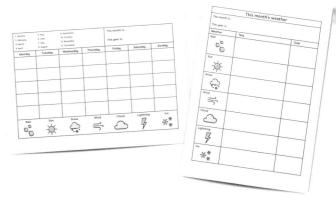

Planning and Timetabling

How we manage planning and timetabling has an immediate and direct impact on how child-led learning is perceived and the value we place on it. Put simply, no matter how well our provision is resourced and organised, if our planning lacks the flexibility to respond to the things children say or do and if our timetable breaks each day into small sections, each with an identified, planned focus, children will not experience the extended periods of time needed to develop ideas in depth.

Access to provision will be piecemeal and children will soon realise that what they choose to do in provision is of less significance than the more formal, adult-led teaching.

Medium and short term planning is essential, but planning too much can restrict our ability to be responsive. If we plan too many activities, our focus will always be on getting through everything, making sure each planned activity happens. This can result in little opportunity for adults to notice and respond to learning as it happens; to share enthusiasm, notice interests, hear and discuss ideas and questions in ways that deepen children's experiences and understanding.

One thing that might help you to rethink your timetable, is to identify lost learning time during each day. Keep track of how many times children break off from their learning (both adult-led and child-led) to line up, go out or come back in and so on. This is a good way to evaluate your current timetable and identify whether changes can be made to maximise time for learning.

In the words of Kath Murdoch:
'...if the daily timetable is fragmented and overcrowded, we easily become driven by the clock rather than our learners. When we feel pressured for time, we literally speed up. We speak faster, we hurry students and give less time for thinking. Distracted by the thought of 'the next thing' we lose the opportunity to be present in THIS moment.'*

Having the flexibility to guide children's learning and respond to their ideas

* Kath Murdoch
Seastar Education Consulting
(2017)

Supporting Children in Provision

An attractive, well-resourced environment as well as time for children to explore it, will not be enough in itself to guarantee quality learning. Adults need to be aware of their role in child-led learning so that children are sufficiently supported.

The first challenge is to ensure that all adults spend time in provision and are not so busy, that all of their time is at a table with a group of children. It's important to feel confident about the multi-faceted nature of teaching which incorporates all our interactions, wherever they occur. Teaching in provision can be as powerful, sometimes more so, than teaching at a table.

The more we know about our children, the more accurate our assessment judgements, and the better we are able to support and extend their learning. By spending time in provision, and discussing children's activities there, you can gather useful information to help you plan what next for children.

So, what do effective interactions with children in provision involve?

– Observing and tuning into the child
– Showing genuine interest in what they are saying and doing
– Respecting their decisions and choices, valuing these
– Helping to re-cap on previous learning
– Reminding how to say or how to hold, or how to share, for example
– Helping a child to clarify and articulate their thinking
– Making suggestions that help move learning forward
– Raising questioning and encouraging children to question

And, deciding not to get involved, if for instance a child is fully focussed and engaged, is equally important.

Challenge and Expectation

The focus on offering sufficient challenge in provision is sometimes misplaced on creating 'Challenges'; activities chosen and set up by the adult in some or all areas of provision, that children are expected to complete.

Whilst there is a place for requiring children to complete these non-negotiables, we need to be aware that these are separate to and different from the activities that children choose to do themselves. Placing challenges in provision, particularly closed challenges, removes the agency children have over what they do and can mean that many children will complete the task superficially, or even avoid the area entirely!

Challenge in provision relates to the decisions you make when planning the areas, the nature of the resources you have included and the organisation as well as the high expectations you set, the way you support and manage behaviour as well as the time given to interacting with children in provision.

Making links in learning

Skilful adults with an in-depth knowledge of the National Curriculum will quickly be able to identify how children's child-led experiences link to aspects of the curriculum, which in turn will help them to be responsive to the needs of the learner, knowing if, when and how to intervene.

Remember too, that child-led learning can also feed into adult-led.

If we focus on the learning objective, the vehicle for teaching a particular concept shouldn't always be determined by the adult. Children being taught to join words and clauses using and, or to use expanded noun phrases, may well be more engaged and have a more extensive bank of ideas to draw from, if they are to write about the construction model they made yesterday or the small world setting they have created.

Similarly, the interest of one child may well provide a highly relevant focus for teaching something specific to a group or the whole class. As long as we are able to accept that this might not fall at the point in the year we had planned, we can still use the opportunity.

Activity 5
Working in Provision

Think with your team about how to ensure children work effectively in provision and are well supported by adults.

- How have your provision areas been introduced to the children?
- How will you ensure that each is working well throughout the year?
- What expectations of children will you put in place and how you will reinforce these regularly?

Consider how your timetable impacts on child-led learning:

- How much time do the children have to access provision?
- Is there a balance between adult-led and child-led?
- Are there extended periods of time, or lots of stop/start?
- How and when do whole class sessions take place?
- Who makes the decisions about which sessions are taught and when?
- How responsive and flexible are you able to be?

With your team, reflect on the adult interactions in your classroom:

- Do staff have time to become involved in children's explorations and talk to them about what they are doing?
- Does information from observations impact on planning?
- Do staff use open questioning to support and extend children, or are they focussed more on 'what' they are doing?
- Are there a range of effective interactions across the environment, or do they happen more in some areas, as opposed to others?
- Are staff confident with sometimes 'saying nothing' and observing instead?

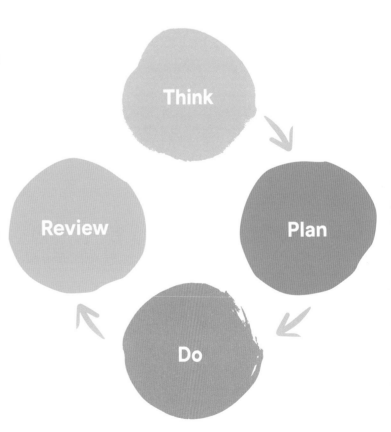

How to Evidence Learning through Continuous Provision

Identifying, discussing and documenting aspects of child-led learning

Work in progress

Evidencing Child-led Learning

Which learning we choose to evidence and how we do this, will reflect on our pedagogical approach. If we view Continuous Provision and the learning opportunities it provides as an integral part of teaching and learning, then we will need to ensure that learning through provision is documented as part of our assessment and observation cycle.

By identifying, discussing and documenting aspects of child-led learning, we give it greater value. This helps children to engage more fully and produce their best efforts, as well as providing good evidence of how provision supports the curriculum.

Ideas for capturing child-led learning include:

- Continuing the Learning Journal approach from EYFS
- Having termly topic books that contain all teaching and learning, both adult and child-led
- Using separate books or folders for child-led evidence
- Having planning books in which children can outline their own ideas for child-initiated activities
- Using a Floor Book for each area of Continuous Provision &/or curriculum subject

You can try a few ideas and then choose the ones that work for you. Whatever you decide to do, paramount is that all learning, whether adult or child-led, is reflected upon and celebrated.

Children's Own Evidence

Often, evidence in Key Stage 1 is provided through children's exercise books and work sheets. These are often used as proof that a child can perform basic skills linked to adult taught language, literacy and maths – sometimes topic work is recorded individually in this way too.

However, enabling children to record their ideas, knowledge and thinking in more creative ways, can reveal far more.

As Julie Fisher* states: 'What children write down will never capture the breadth and depth of their current knowledge, because at 5, 6 and 7, children's writing skills are not sufficiently developed.

Children's thinking is way in advanced of their writing skills. The only useful evidence that writing can provide is that of writing development.'

As children move through Key Stage 1, we can gradually extend the expectations we have of them, making recording their learning an integral part of the process of learning through self-led or adult-led enquiry. Rather than an adult-imposed add on, perhaps a worksheet, we can provide both clear structures and a bank of approaches that children can use. Here are four aspects for you to consider.

Capturing child-led learning with Floor Books

* Moving On to Key Stage 1,
Julie Fisher
Open University Press
(2020)

Planning Ideas

In tune with children's developmental changes and the progress of their learning, planning for what they have in mind and want to do moves from a short discussion to an increasingly sophisticated and detailed recorded process with children encouraged and supported to shape their ideas through discussion, drawing, diagrams or writing.

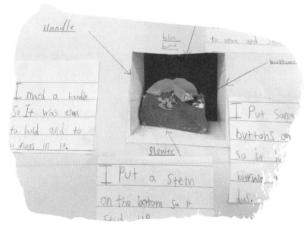

Reviewing Progress

As well as extended periods of time in which to follow their ideas through, children will need to be given sufficient time and encouragement to focus on the progress of their work and consider what their next steps might be. Establishing and embedding small group or whole class review times is extremely valuable.

These sessions are much more than 'show-and-tell'. Often, the learning reviewed is selected by the adult for the purpose of focussing on specific, curriculum-related learning objectives or on a particular child/children. These sessions are planned as an opportunity to challenge and extend children's ideas, develop their vocabulary, and help them solve problems. They are occasions for revisiting and introducing skills and knowledge as well as key learning behaviours, and to reiterate expectations regarding the quality of learning.

Evaluating Learning

As children continue to work with Continuous Provision through Key Stage 1, they need to effectively evaluate and improve their work with increasing independence and challenge.

In the way that we introduce success criteria for a writing genre, so too can we set clear expectations for learning in Continuous Provision. Success criteria help to motivate children to do their best and provide a frame of reference for adults to challenge children and reiterate high expectations, whilst providing the support they need to reach them.

There is no need to introduce extensive lists of expectations to every area all at the same time as this will be overwhelming and unachievable. Instead, consider when and what is appropriate for your children and how taught concepts can be reflected.

Planning and documenting ideas in a range of ways

* With thanks to All Saints CofE Infant & Pre-School, Huthwaite, Sutton-In-Ashfield, Nottinghamshire for the images shared in this section

Presenting Learning

Finally, we need to reflect on how children can present their thinking, what they've been exploring and finding out about.

Opportunities to share learning might include:

- Presentations: develop a more structured approach, in line with the expectations of the spoken language elements of the National Curriculum
- Galleries & Displays: show progression from adding a name label through to including dates, title, captions and descriptions
- Writing in Books: lists, instructions and recounts that make links to taught concepts
- Diagrams and annotated photographs

Within each of these aspects of the learning process, we need to consider how to secure progression through the year and across the Key Stage. It is worth spending time thinking about what you want to see your children doing by the end of the year as this will enable you to plan out the steps needed to achieve this, identifying as you do what skills and concepts will need to be taught and embedded.

Eventually, children can be supported to make decisions about how they intend to share their work, at the planning stage. Expectations regarding the ways they do this can also be gradually extended.

For example, a group of children focussing on the life cycle of turtles, may work towards:

- Creating a 3D model with moving parts
- Creating a 2D piece of art
- Compiling a fact sheet
- Creating and presenting a PowerPoint presentation

Activity 6
Capturing Learning in Provision

Consider how well your environment, routines and approaches to teaching enable children to plan, evaluate and record their learning.

- How does your environment support independent recording?
- Are resources available that children can use to record in different ways?
- Have the children been taught how to use them?
- What recording methods have been previously taught?
- What skills could they apply from previously taught sessions?

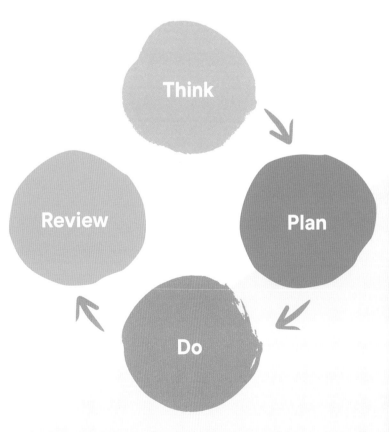

Continuous Provision Planning Guides KS1

Four Step Planning Process

1 Study the How to Guide

2 Choose an area to review

3 Read through the EEx Guide for this area

4 With your team, talk about your own area and create your own plan

Guide to Continuous Provision in KS1

Maths Area

Early Excellence
Inspirational Learning

Learning Intentions Y1/Y2/KS1 National Curriculum

Number

– Count to and across 100, forwards and backwards, beginning with 0 or 1, or from any given number
– Count, read and write numbers to 100 in numerals *and words*; count in multiples of twos, fives, tens *and threes*
– *Recognise the place value of each digit in a two-digit number (tens, ones)*
– Identify and represent numbers using objects and pictorial representations including the number line, and use the language of: equal to, more than, less than (fewer), most, least
– Read and write numbers from 1 to 20/ *at least 100* in numerals and words
– Solve problems that involve addition and subtraction including *with two-digit numbers* using addition, subtraction and equals signs
– Solve problems involving multiplication and division, *and write them using multiplication, division and equals signs*
– *Apply their increasing knowledge of mental and written methods*
– Recognise, find and name a half and a quarter of an object, shape or quantity *and write fractions 1/3, 1/4, 2/4, 3/4 of a length, shape, set or quantity*

Shape, Space & Measure

– Compare, describe and solve practical problems for lengths/heights, mass/weight, capacity/volume and time; *measure, estimate and begin to record using appropriate standard units*
– Begin to measure the above, *using appropriate standard units to estimate and measure to the nearest appropriate unit, using rulers, scales, thermometers and measuring vessels*
– *Use the signs >, < and = to compare and order measurements*
– Tell the time to the hour, half past the hour *and to five minutes*
– Recognise and name common 2D and 3D shapes
– *Compare and sort common 2D and 3D shapes and everyday objects*
– *Order and arrange combinations of mathematical objects in patterns and sequences*

English

– Ask relevant questions to extend their understanding and knowledge
– Articulate and justify answers, arguments and opinions
– Use spoken language to develop understanding through speculating, hypothesising, imagining and exploring ideas
– Form digits 0-9

Science

– Ask simple questions and recognise that they can be answered in different ways
– Observe closely, using simple equipment
– Perform simple tests
– Gather and record data to help in answering questions

Learning Behaviours

Dispositions & Attitudes

– Making decisions about the resources needed and how to proceed
– Investigating and exploring concepts through the use of manipulatives
– Engaging with new contexts and ideas, responding to challenges and solving problems
– Making links between areas of learning
– Collaborating with peers, sharing resources and engaging in purposeful conversations
– Planning and communicating their mathematical ideas, through the use of resources, verbally and in written/pictorial form
– Being resourceful and independent

– Learning objectives introduced in yr2

KS1 Practice & Provision / Teaching & Learning

Experience Offered

- Counting by lining up or grouping objects including in multiples, matching amounts to wooden numbers or recording on whiteboards
- Sharing objects equally between bowls
- Creating and continuing number lines and number sentences with numbered objects or small numbers
- Identifying and describing patterns on a 100 square
- Building and ordering 2 & 3 digit numbers using the wooden numerals
- Sorting and organising objects including shapes, into hoops according to chosen criteria
- Creating and continuing patterns and repeating arrangements of objects and numbers, including reflective ones
- Playing challenge games e.g. find the number on the 100 square 'Find ten more than 23…' or pick up pairs to ten
- Inventing and playing board games, recording instructions and rules and keeping score
- Using the dice and spinners in a variety of ways e.g. adding or subtracting two numbers thrown, deciding which gives the best result for the game being played
- Draw around shapes on whiteboard grids, counting how many squares are inside the shape
- Measuring, recording and ordering length, weight, capacity and time including as part of learning in other areas of provision
- Sharing mathematical ideas with peers and adults, using taught mathematical language and terminology
- Reading and sharing books, discussing and responding to the maths ideas represented

Enhancement Ideas

- Books, both fiction and non-fiction with mathematical themes
- Images of maths in the natural or made environment, including from familiar places
- Materials displaying numbers and prices such as calendars, diaries, telephone directories, brochures, sale advertisement leaflets
- Real life equipment that incorporate numbers such as mobile phone, till, calculator
- A selection of boxes and containers of various kinds, including those formed from complex nets
- Traditional or historical games such as Solitaire, Mancala or Ludo

Resource Organisation

- A distinct area with open shelving, table and chairs
- Resources grouped together by theme or criteria
- Resources organised into open pots, shallow trays, baskets or boxes
- Larger resources sorted by size, numerical order or specific visual arrangement, silhouetted onto the shelves to support shape recognition and maintenance of the area
- Resources clearly labelled using text and photographs as appropriate
- Number of items or capacity included on labels/shelves

Key Resources

- Range of natural materials and small world creatures for sorting & counting including in 2s, 5s & 10s
- Bowls & hoops to support counting & calculating
- Number & calculation symbol cards and number lines
- Numbered items such as pebbles or bean bags and small wooden numbers
- A set of number cards and lines
- Write-on tens frames
- Set of write-on 100 squares including some that are blank
- Plain and gridded whiteboards and whiteboard pens
- Blank games boards and a variety of dice and spinners that include larger numbers, numerals and symbols
- Variety of objects that can be used as counters or tokens
- Calculator
- A set of small 2D and 3D shapes and mirrors
- A range of sand timers, stop watches and a small clock
- A variety of tape measures including metre and longer and 30cm rulers (cm only)
- Weighing scales including balance, kitchen and digital and a set of spring balances
- A range of bottles and containers with marked scales including litre containers of different shapes
- Books with a maths theme

Vocabulary

Number, count on/up/to/from/ down, before, after, forwards, backwards, one more, one less, equal to, more, less, many, few, fewer, least, fewest, smallest, greater, less, most, odd, even

Ones, tens, hundreds, value, digit, partition, part, whole order, compare, pattern

Calculate, number sentence, put together, add, altogether, total, take away, subtract, share, multiply, group, array, left over, double, halve, distance between, difference between, equal, same, less than, greater than

Fraction, half, quarter, whole, part

Full, half full, empty, weigh, weighs, balances, heavy, heavier, heaviest, light, lighter, lightest

Quick, quicker, quickest, quickly , fast, faster, fastest, slow, slower, slowest, slowly, quicker, slower, earlier, later, hour, minute, second, o'clock, half past, clockface, watch, hands

Cube, cuboid, pyramid, sphere, cone, cylinder, circle, triangle, square, shape, flat, curved, straight, round, hollow, solid, corner (point, pointed), face, side, edge

Recording Opportunities

- Labelling the groups and sets that are decided upon
- Recording their problem solving in words and pictures e.g. drawing objects shared between a number of bowls
- Writing numerals
- Recording the rules and scores for invented games
- Pictorial representations of patterns and calculation problems and approaches
- Recording number sentences

Engage with **@earlyexcellence** on our social media channels & visit
earlyexcellence.com/subscribe to receive the latest updates

© Early Excellence Ltd 2021

43

Block Area

Learning Intentions Y1/Y2/KS1 National Curriculum

English

- Listen and respond appropriately to adults and their peers
- Ask relevant questions to extend their understanding and knowledge
- Use spoken language to develop understanding through speculating, hypothesising, imagining and exploring ideas
- Write sentences, captions and labels using taught concepts and structures
- Begin to form letters correctly, starting and finishing in the right place
- Develop a positive attitude and stamina for writing
- Write for a range of different purposes
- Write sentences by saying out loud what they are going to write about
- *Write down ideas and/or key words, including new vocabulary*
- Re-read what they have written to check that it makes sense
- Discuss what they have written with the teacher or other pupils
- *Read aloud what they have written with appropriate intonation to make the meaning clear*
- Apply simple spelling rules and guidance, as listed in English Appendices 1 & 2

Maths

- Read numbers to 100 in numerals and words, write numbers to 20 in words; count in multiples of twos, fives, tens *and threes, forward and backward*
- Given a number, identify one more and one less
- *Solve problems involving multiplication and division, using arrays/ repeated addition, including problems in contexts*
- Recognise, find and name a half as one of two equal parts and a quarter as one of four equal parts of an object, shape or quantity *and also write fractions 1/3, 1/4, 2/4, 3/4*
- Recognise and name common 2D and 3D shapes *and identify 2D shapes on the surface of 3D shapes*
- *Compare and sort common 2D and 3D shapes and everyday objects*

Science

- Distinguish between an object and the material from which it is made
- Identify and name everyday materials
- Describe the simple physical properties of a variety of everyday materials
- Compare and group a variety of everyday materials on the basis of their properties
- *Identify and compare the suitability of a variety of everyday materials for particular uses*

Geography

- Use basic geographical vocabulary to refer to key physical features, including: beach, cliff, coast, forest, hill, mountain, sea, ocean, river, soil, valley, vegetation, season and weather
- Use basic geographical vocabulary to refer to key human features, including: city, town, village, factory, farm, house, office, port, harbour and shop
- Use simple compass directions (North, South, East and West) and locational and directional language [for example, near and far; left and right], to describe the location of features and routes on a map
- Use aerial photographs and plan perspectives to recognise landmarks and basic human and physical features
- Devise simple maps, use and construct basic symbols in a key

Design & Technology

- Generate, develop, model and communicate their ideas through talking and mock-ups
- Evaluate their ideas and products against design criteria
- Build structures, exploring how they can be made stronger, stiffer and more stable

History

- Learn about significant historical places in their own locality

Learning Behaviours

Dispositions & Attitudes

- Making decisions and informed choices about the resources they need
- Cooperating effectively and share resources appropriately
- Planning and communicating ideas, thinking ahead to complete each step of their idea
- Adapting and modifying their ideas to achieve their result
- Trying different approaches
- Including a wider range of materials to enhance their block play e.g. paper/card for building fronts and architectural details
- Using a growing range of interesting and appropriate vocabulary
- Critically reflecting on progress and outcome of their ideas
- Taking responsibility for the organisation of the area

– Learning objectives introduced in yr2

KS1 Practice & Provision / Teaching & Learning

Key Resources

- A selection of wooden blocks and shapes including mathematically regular shapes
- A selection of flat boards and small planks of differing sizes, shapes and thickness
- A selection of natural wooden pieces
- Tools to support building and recording such as rulers, tape measures, spirit levels, clipboards, squared paper, notebooks and pens
- Enhancements linked to themes or interests e.g. books and images

Resource Organisation

- Regular shaped blocks silhouetted onto the shelf in arrays or by size order
- Photographs and/or text for labels linked to the name of the resource
- Mathematical language used for labelling with numerals/arrays/ repeated addition/multiplication/fractions
- Resources grouped together according to their characteristics e.g. buttons, cotton reels, beads

Experience Offered

- Create imaginative and real-world settings
- Design a landscape for a story or particular character
- Draw and labelling a map of own setting/landscape
- Take an aerial photograph of your setting/landscape
- Build a bridge from...to...
- Build a town containing...
- Build a structure only using shapes with a curved edge, for example
- Write instructions for how to build...

Vocabulary

Mathematical
Edge, centre, corner, group, sort, cube, cuboid, pyramid, sphere, cone, cylinder, circle, triangle, square, shape, flat, curved, straight, round, hollow, solid, corner, point, pointed, face, side, edge, make, build, draw, whole, equal parts, four equal parts, one half, two halves, a quarter, two quarters, start at, look at, point to, put, place, fit

Geographical
Position, over, under, underneath, above, below, top, bottom, side on, in, outside, inside, around, in front, behind, front, back, before, after, beside, next to, opposite, apart, between, middle

Scientific
Equipment, identify, assess, force, balance, greater than, smaller than, equal to, question, answer, guess, predict, conclude

D&T
Shape, join, construct, design, evaluate, amend, build, process, product, measure, mark out, assemble, materials, kits, 3D, 2D

Recording Opportunities

- Create labels and signs for buildings
- Label maps with place names and symbols
- Photograph buildings during progress and when completed or making short films
- Create a set of instructions to explain to a friend how to build it
- Take an aerial photograph of a building or place they have made
- Create a map of their setting
- Complete planning sheets

Enhancement Ideas

- Fiction and non-fiction books that focus on children's interests or current themes
- Photographs or drawings of buildings and structures, including those that are well known to the children
- Images or designs of particular details for example doors or architectural ornaments
- Aerial photographs and maps of real and imaginative settings
- Resources to support writing including large pieces of paper to build onto or caption cards to note narrative details as well as gridded paper for map making
- Additional blocks such as those including coloured/patterned shapes, or unusual and challenging multi-faceted blocks

Engage with @earlyexcellence on our social media channels & visit
earlyexcellence.com/subscribe to receive the latest updates

© Early Excellence Ltd 2021

45

Continuous Provision Planning Guide KS1

Small World Area

 Early Excellence
Inspirational Learning

Learning Intentions Y1/Y2/KS1 National Curriculum

English

– Listen and respond appropriately to adults and their peers
– Ask relevant questions to extend their understanding and knowledge
– Articulate and justify answers, arguments and opinions
– Give well-structured descriptions, explanations and narratives for different purposes, including for expressing feelings
– Maintain attention and participate actively in collaborative conversations, staying on topic and initiating and responding to comments
– Use spoken language to develop understanding through speculating, hypothesising, imagining and exploring ideas
– Consider and evaluate different viewpoints, attending to and building on the contributions of others
– Become familiar with and retell key stories, fairy stories and traditional tales retelling them and considering their particular characteristics
– Write sentences, captions and labels using taught concepts and structures
– Apply simple spelling rules and guidance, as listed in English Appendices 1 & 2

Science

– Identify and classify
– Identify and name a variety of common animals including fish, amphibians, reptiles, birds and mammals
– Identify and name a variety of common animals that are carnivores, herbivores and omnivores
– *Identify and name a variety of animals in their habitats*

Relationships Education

– Know that others' families, either in school or in the wider world, sometimes look different from their family, but that they should respect those differences and know that other children's families are also characterised by love and care

Maths

– Count, read and write numbers in numerals *and in words*
– Sequence events in chronological order using language [for example, before and after, next, first, today, yesterday, tomorrow, morning, afternoon and evening]

Learning Behaviours

Dispositions & Attitudes

– Making decisions and informed choices about the resources they need
– Expressing their thoughts and ideas to other
– Co-operating effectively and sharing resources appropriately
– Planning and communicating ideas, thinking ahead to complete each step of their idea
– Using a growing range of interesting and appropriate vocabulary
– Critically reflecting on progress and outcome of their ideas
– Taking responsibility for the organisation of the area and care of resources

– Learning objectives introduced in yr2

KS1 Practice & Provision / Teaching & Learning

Key Resources

- A selection of natural resources, e.g. fir cones, shells, pebbles
- Decorative resources and fabric to represent landscapes and add detail
- A diverse range of small world people including differing ages, ethnicities and abilities
- A selection of fantasy figures including king/prince, queen/princess, witch/wizard, knights & dragon
- A number of open-ended 'block people' in different colours
- A collection of small world animals supporting scientific/geographical learning including reptiles, amphibians, mammals, fish & birds from different continents/habitats
- Tools to support recording such as clipboards, post it notes, caption strips, notebooks and pens
- Enhancements including books and photographs linked to themes or children's interests e.g. books, images, additional small world figures

Resource Organisation

- Collections of resources sorted and displayed in plastic trays, grouped together according to their characteristics e.g. fabric, natural resources, glass gems
- Trays grouped together by theme e.g. landscapes, characters, people, animals
- Small world animals organised by scientific or geographical criteria such as habitat, continent, mammals/reptiles
- Photographs, labels and lists of the animals included, supporting vocabulary re above details

Experience Offered

- Retell familiar stories and develop story themes and ideas
- Narrate their play
- Create imaginative and real-world scenarios and narratives
- Invent stories with a beginning, middle and end
- Write labels or captions for characters and events
- Find ways to record their ideas and stories in images and text
- Experiment with and use a range of vocabulary to describe their ideas and stories
- Use descriptive language to describe settings and characters

Vocabulary

English
Character, setting, plot, beginning, middle, end, first, next, then, last, after that, after a while, finally, eventually, meanwhile

Science
Classify, group, sort, compare, contrast, describe, mammal, reptile, amphibian, fish, bird, carnivore, omnivore, herbivore, food chain, young, adult, habitat

Maths
Before, after, next, first, today, yesterday, tomorrow, morning, afternoon, evening

Recording Opportunities

- Create labels and signs for settings, characters and plot developments
- Photograph beginning, middle and end of stories or make a short film
- Use photographs or drawings to make a book of their story; read the story to others
- Take an aerial photograph of a setting
- Create a labeled map of a setting
- Complete story maps or plans

Enhancement Ideas

- Fiction and non-fiction books that focus on children's interests or current class themes
- Additional small world creatures or characters that reflect class books, themes or children's interests
- Small world figures and natural resources that relate to the current season
- Photographs and artistic representations of real and imaginative settings
- Maps and aerial photographs of a range of landscapes
- Resources to further support writing, map making and large-scale story mapping, including large sheets of paper

Engage with @earlyexcellence on our social media channels & visit
earlyexcellence.com/subscribe to receive the latest updates

© Early Excellence Ltd 2021

47

Construction Area

Learning Intentions Y1/Y2/KS1 National Curriculum

English

- Listen and respond appropriately to adults and their peers
- Ask relevant questions to extend their understanding and knowledge
- Give well-structured descriptions, explanations and narratives for different purposes, including for expressing opinions
- Write sentences, captions and labels using taught concepts and structures
- Apply simple spelling rules and guidance, as listed in English Appendices 1 & 2
- Re-read what they have written to check that it makes sense

Maths

- Compare, describe and solve practical problems for lengths and heights [for example, long/short, longer/shorter, tall/short, double/half]
- Measure and begin to record lengths and heights
- *Choose and use appropriate standard units to estimate and measure length/height in any direction*
- *Compare and order lengths*
- Sequence events in chronological order using language [for example, before and after, next and first]

Science

- Distinguish between an object and the material from which it is made
- Describe the simple physical properties of a variety of everyday materials
- Compare and group together a variety of everyday materials on the basis of their simple physical properties.

Art & Design

- Learn about the work of a range of artists, craft makers and designers, making links to their own work

Design & Technology

- Design purposeful, functional, appealing products for themselves and other users based on design criteria
- Generate, develop, model and communicate their ideas through talking, drawing, templates, mock-ups and, where appropriate, information and communication technology
- Select from and use a wide range of materials and components, including construction materials, according to their characteristics
- Evaluate their ideas and products against design criteria
- Build structures, exploring how they can be made stronger, stiffer and more stable
- Explore and use mechanisms [for example, levers, sliders, wheels and axles], in their products

Learning Behaviours

Dispositions & Attitudes

- Generating ideas based on their own interests and ideas or simple design criteria
- Planning and developing their ideas through drawings and mock-ups
- Making and explaining decisions about the resources they need
- Co-operating with peers and sharing resources
- Expressing and explaining their thoughts and ideas to others
- Adapting and modifying their ideas, using trial and error
- Reflecting on the progress and outcome of their ideas including its intended purpose, when appropriate

– Learning objectives introduced in yr2

KS1 Practice & Provision / Teaching & Learning

Key Resources

- A small number of age appropriate construction kits e.g. Brio, that offer a range of different ways to connect
- A range of wheels in different sizes
- A selection of dowelling rods
- A selection of caps and spacers that fit the rods
- A selection of beads and threading laces or lengths of string
- A range of building equipment such as spirit levels, measuring tapes and rulers
- A set of recording equipment such as gridded whiteboards, clipboards and pens
- A selection of books to support construction ideas

Resource Organisation

- Collections of resources sorted and displayed in shallow plastic trays
- Resources grouped and arranged according to the type of resource and its purpose e.g. connectors, rods, beads
- Trays or carryall to store resources for measurement and recording
- Photographs and/or text for labels linked to the name of the resource or part
- Some resources e.g. doweling rods, labelled according to length
- A space nearby for children to safely store and return to their unfinished models
- A space for children to display their finished models

Experience Offered

- Create real and imagined buildings and structures of increasing complexity including with moving parts
- Make products that incorporate mechanisms such as wheels, winding reels, hinges and levers
- Follow instructions involving several stages of construction in images &/or text
- Talk about their ideas
- Draw and/or label their designs and/or create maps of their buildings and structures
- Measure the size, shape and balance of their designs
- Develop and communicate their ideas, finding ways to record and share their ideas
- Experiment with and use a range of vocabulary to describe their designs and ideas
- Use mathematical, descriptive, scientific and geographical language to describe their buildings and structures
- Review and evaluate their work and make improvements

Vocabulary

Design & Technology
Plan, design, investigate, product, function, dismantle, connect, structure, engineer, evaluate, axle, lever, hinge, mechanism, stable, level, purpose, instructions, order, criteria, mock-up

Science
Wood, bamboo, plastic, metal, solid, bendy, stretchy

English
First, next, then, last, after that

Recording Opportunities

- Plan their products in drawn and/or written form
- Create labels and signs for their displayed models
- Produce labelled diagrams of their products
- Create instructions for their products that others can follow using images and text

Enhancement Ideas

- Fiction and non-fiction books that focus on children's interests or current themes
- Photographs or diagrams of structures made using the resources provided, including some by other children
- Instruction leaflets for the resources provided, as well as other structures, such as flat-pack furniture
- Photographs of structures such as truss bridges, vehicles, and sculptures
- Close up images and/or diagrams of engineering details such as struts, roof joists or axels
- Small scale models or artefacts that demonstrate key principles such as clock or machine parts, moving toys

Engage with **@earlyexcellence** on our social media channels & visit
earlyexcellence.com/subscribe to receive the latest updates

© Early Excellence Ltd 2021

49

Writing Area

Early Excellence
Inspirational Learning

Learning Intentions Y1/Y2/KS1 National Curriculum

English

- Listen and respond appropriately to adults and their peers
- Ask relevant questions to extend their understanding and knowledge
- Use spoken language to develop understanding through speculating, hypothesising, imagining and exploring ideas
- Write sentences, captions and labels using taught concepts and structures
- Begin to form letters correctly, starting and finishing in the right place, *using some strokes to join letters, correctly sizing capital letters and digits and spacing between words that reflects the size of the letter*
- Develop a positive attitude and stamina for writing
- Write for a range of different purposes
- *Write narratives about personal experiences and those of others (real and fictional); about real events; poetry*
- Write sentences by saying out loud what they are going to write about
- *Plan or say out loud what they are going to write about*
- *Write down ideas and/or key words, including new vocabulary; encapsulate what they want to say, sentence by sentence*
- *Re-read what they have written to check that it makes sense, and that verbs to indicate time are used correctly and consistently, including verbs in the continuous form*
- *Proof-read their writing to check for errors in spelling, grammar and punctuation*
- Discuss/evaluate what they have written with the teacher or other pupils

Maths

- Read numbers from 1 to 20/ to at least 100 in numerals and words
- Use/recall and use fluently, number bonds and related subtraction facts within 20

Design & Technology

- Select from and use a range of tools and equipment to perform practical tasks [for example, cutting, shaping, joining and finishing]

Learning Behaviours

Dispositions & Attitudes

- Making decisions and informed choices about the resources they need
- Expressing their thoughts and ideas to others with increasing clarity
- Cooperating effectively and share resources appropriately
- Planning and communicating ideas, thinking ahead to complete each step of their idea
- Using a growing range of interesting and appropriate vocabulary
- Critically reflecting on progress and outcome of their ideas
- Taking responsibility for the organisation of the area and care of resources

– Learning objectives introduced in yr2

KS1 Practice & Provision / Teaching & Learning

Key Resources

- A variety of writing materials including biros, gel pens, felt-tips, pencil crayons, chalk/chalk-pens, dry-wipe pens, highlighters
- A variety of paper and card in various shapes, sizes, colours and thicknesses including plain and lined paper, sticky notes and labels
- A small selection of joining equipment and tools including scissors (left & right handed), hole punch, treasury tags, paper clips, stapler, staples and glue
- A small number of clipboards and dry-wipe boards (including a wall mounted board if available) including some that are lined
- Display stands for card and whiteboards
- A selection of writing/phonic resources including line guides, alphabet strips/arcs, upper and lower-case letters, high frequency words on cards/pebbles/mats
- Appropriate phonics resources including phoneme mats/cards
- Relevant handwriting resources/cues
- Resources to support the creation of narratives e.g. cards featuring characters, setting and key objects/events
- Taught frames/scaffolds for story maps, plans, instructions etc
- Prompts for writing such as artefacts and high-quality images
- Instructions re how to make small books
- Voice recorders
- Simple dictionary, thesaurus and spelling guide

Resource Organisation

- Table and chairs in an easily accessible area of the classroom
- Open shelving to store resources
- Large whiteboard available, if possible
- Space to display children's completed writing
- Pens and pencils sorted into pots
- Cutting and joining tools stored together in a box/basket
- Small resources e.g. lower case letters, grouped and stored together in small boxes
- Paper, labels, whiteboards grouped and stored in shallow trays
- Resources clearly labelled with text (and photographs if appropriate), some referencing number in numeral or word form or key number facts

Experience Offered

- Write for a wide variety of purposes, in a wide range of styles (prompts and resources to support newly taught approaches added to provision, as appropriate), documenting familiar experiences/narratives and developing imaginative stories
- Creating books, cards, letters, invitations and notes
- Practising and revisiting taught spelling and grammar concepts
- Putting phonics and grammar knowledge into practice
- Practising writing skills; improving their tripod grip and developing fluency
- Writing with increasing stamina and concentration
- Planning their writing before beginning by listing ideas or key vocabulary
- Read aloud what they have written to themselves, a peer or adult, checking that it makes sense
- Proof-read for accuracy, making changes and improvements with increasing independence

Vocabulary

English
Suffix, prefix, verb, adjective, word, sentence, plural, describe, setting, character, plot, sentence, punctuation, writer, author, illustrator, publisher, text, illustration, vocabulary, once, then, next, after that, at last, finally, in the end, when, if, that, but, because, or, the next day, soon, plan, plan, check, improve

Design & Technology
Plan, join, mechanism, flap, tab, insert, slot, instructions

Recording Opportunities

- Writing in different genres including narratives, recounts, non-chronological reports, instructions, explanations, invitations, lists, plans, letters, information texts
- Planning and drafting writing
- Producing and presenting final drafts
- Developing different ways of recording and documenting their experiences and ideas
- Writing opportunities linked to other provision areas e.g. role play or classroom routines/procedures
- Creating signs and labels for provision areas or classroom displays
- Create forms or charts for use during child led learning e.g. appointment cards, as well as for the organisation or maintenance of provision areas e.g. listing fruit available/selected that week

Enhancement Ideas

- Examples of writing done by others and images of them as they write for different purposes, including authors, members of the school community and authors
- Message collection and delivery points e.g. post boxes or individual message centres
- Different or unusual writing tools, boards and papers
- Materials to support a variety of writing opportunities including notebooks, shopping lists, diaries or forms to complete
- Intriguing images, story strips or artefacts
- A selection of small objects such as gemstones, a wand, an old key or map to prompt narratives

Engage with **@earlyexcellence** on our social media channels & visit
earlyexcellence.com/subscribe to receive the latest updates

Books & Puppets Area

Early Excellence
Inspirational Learning

Learning Intentions Y1/Y2/KS1 National Curriculum

English

– Listen and respond appropriately to adults and their peers
– Participate in discussions, presentations, performances, role play, improvisations
– Gain, maintain and monitor the interest of the listener(s)
– Apply their growing phonic knowledge and skills to decode words, *until automatic decoding has become embedded and reading is fluent*
– Read aloud books closely matched to their developing phonic knowledge, *sounding out unfamiliar words accurately, automatically and without undue hesitation*
– Re-read books to build fluency and confidence
– Develop pleasure in reading, motivation to read, vocabulary and understanding
– Become familiar with and retell a wider range of stories, fairy stories, traditional tales
– Learn to appreciate rhymes and poems, and to recite some by heart, *continuing to build up a repertoire*
– Check that the text makes sense to them as they read, correcting inaccurate reading
– *Participate in discussions about books, poems and other works, taking turns and listening to what others say*

Relationships Education

– Know that others' families, either in school or in the wider world, sometimes look different from their family, and know that other children's families are also characterised by love and care
– Know that stable, caring relationships, which may be of different types, are at the heart of happy families, and are important for children's security as they grow up
– Recognise the characteristics of friendships, including mutual respect, truthfulness, trustworthiness, loyalty, kindness, generosity, trust, sharing interests and experiences and support with problems and difficulties

Learning Behaviours

Dispositions & Attitudes

– Making informed choices about the texts they read
– Expressing their thoughts and ideas to other
– Cooperating effectively and sharing resources appropriately
– Using a growing range of interesting and appropriate vocabulary
– Critically reflecting on what they read, including making links to other texts
– Taking responsibility for the organisation of the area and care of resources
– Developing ways to record and feedback their opinions and responses

– Learning objectives introduced in yr2

Key Resources	Resource Organisation	Experience Offered
English / Teaching & Learning – A CD player or media player with headphones to allow children to listen to texts read aloud – A selection of fiction texts, poetry & rhyme including: favourite/familiar texts; hardback & paperback texts; books with a variety of illustrative styles; books that are diverse and inclusive and from a range of different cultures; books that challenge and stretch in terms of theme and plot; stories with predictable and patterned language; traditional fairy tales; stories about fantasy worlds; stories with familiar settings; different stories by the same author – A selection of puppets linked to popular story themes (these may be displayed in an adjoining area, if space allows) e.g. farm and wild animals, people & fantasy characters	– A rug or carpeted area with cushions/comfy seating in a quieter area of the room – Sloping book shelf or open shelving with bookstands – A small display area to display a focus book or author – A selection of books displayed facing forwards – Additional books grouped by theme such as favourite stories stored in accessible boxes or baskets – Focus book(s) displayed on separate shelf or low table along with relevant information, artefacts or images – Puppet area close to or within the book area to be used in a puppet theatre or carpeted area – Collections of puppets (including any made by the children) stored and displayed in baskets or on individual stands – Writing resources including whiteboards and pens, or a large, child height whiteboard or large sheets of paper	– Selecting and handling books carefully and appropriately – Sharing books and puppets and their responses to these, with others – Listening to and concentrating on a story read by adults or their peers, joining in with repeated phrases, asking questions discussing aspects of the story/poem – Reading, retelling and enjoying new and familiar texts on their own, showing focus and concentration – Reading a range of texts with increasing independence and fluency, including some that link to progress in phonics – Expressing related experiences and imaginative ideas – Using puppets to act out story ideas and familiar experiences – Creating plots around a set of characters, using and experimenting with a growing range of vocabulary to explain their ideas and tell their stories

Vocabulary	Recording Opportunities	Enhancement Ideas
English Fiction, non-fiction, chapter, page, story, setting, character, characteristics, personality, behaviour, plot, beginning, middle, end, description, poem, rhyme, line, opinion, discuss, like, dislike, prefer, fairy tale, traditional tale, illustration, illustrator **Relationships Education** Family, relationship, difference, feeling, emotion, safe, unsafe, trust, respect, friendship, friendly	– Note responses to books read e.g. by writing name when they have read/shared a book; indicate preferences of text/character by adding to tick-list/tally chart or similar (these could be set up and collated by children) – Comment on aspects of the focus book such as plot or illustrations in floorbook, on comment cards or sticky notes – Note new, unfamiliar or interesting vocabulary or ideas to explore and share with others – Plan characters and roles to be taken when developing a puppet show – Plan and write a script for a puppet show – Crete signs, advertising and so on, to accompany a performance	– Fiction texts including poetry with a common theme or by a particular author – Books and images with the same illustrator or illustrative style – Small world resources or puppets that link to current focus book(s) – Opportunities to respond to the books read in simple ways, by moving a counter or adding to a tally chart for example – Equipment for children to record themselves reading a book, interviewing a friend or creating a character's voice – A puppet theatre for puppets provided or made by the children

Engage with @earlyexcellence on our social media channels & visit
earlyexcellence.com/subscribe to receive the latest updates

© Early Excellence Ltd 2021

53

Role Play Area

Learning Intentions Y1/Y2/KS1 National Curriculum

English

- Listen and respond appropriately to adults and their peers
- Maintain attention and participate actively in collaborative conversations, staying on topic and initiating and responding to comments
- Participate in role play
- Use spoken language to develop understanding through speculating, hypothesising, imagining and exploring ideas
- Gain, maintain and monitor the interest of the listener(s)
- Consider and evaluate different viewpoints, attending to and building on the contributions of others
- Select and use appropriate registers for effective communication
- Write for a range of different purposes including signs & lists using taught spelling and sentence concepts
- Re-read what they have written to check that it makes sense

Maths

- Count, read and write numbers in numerals and in words
- Solve one-step problems that involve addition and subtraction, using concrete objects
- Compare, describe and solve practical problems for lengths/heights, mass/weight and time
- Measure and begin to record lengths & heights, time
- *Choose and use appropriate standard units to estimate and measure length & height*
- Recognise and know the value of different denominations or coins & notes
- *Recognise and use symbols for pounds (£) and pence (p); combine amounts to make a particular value*
- *Solve simple problems in a practical context involving addition and subtraction of money of the same unit, including giving change*
- Recognise and use language relating to dates, including days of the week
- Tell the time to the hour and half past the hour/to five minutes, *including quarter past/to the hour and draw the hands on a clock face to show these times*

History

- Learn about changes within living memory and significant historical events, people and places in their own locality

Relationship Education

- Know the characteristics of healthy family life
- Know that others' families sometimes look different from their family, but that they should respect those differences
- Know how important friendships are in making us feel happy and secure, and how people choose and make friends
- Understand the characteristics of friendships
- Know the importance of respecting others and the conventions of courtesy and manners

Learning Behaviours

Dispositions & Attitudes

- Playing alongside others, communicating, sharing ideas, negotiating and co-operating
- Learning from and valuing other people's ideas
- Making decisions and informed choices about the resources they need
- Expressing their thoughts and ideas to other
- Planning and communicate ideas, including in writing, thinking ahead to complete each step of their idea
- Introducing their play to their peers, explaining contexts and procedures
- Reading and writing for a variety of purposes and in different real-life and imaginative contexts
- Using a growing range of interesting and appropriate vocabulary
- Critically reflecting on progress and outcome of their ideas
- Managing and organising resources, getting things out and tidying away
- Using money to role play exchanging money for items
- Taking responsibility for the organisation of the area and care of resources

– Learning objectives introduced in yr2

KS1 Practice & Provision / Teaching & Learning

Key Resources

- A space for open-ended role play
- A frame with large pegs and a selection of large fabric pieces to create settings and backdrops
- A small table and chairs
- A variety of everyday clothes such as jackets, ties, waistcoats and hats
- A selection of real-life work uniforms such as police, vet, doctor and scientist
- A range of real-life props such as stethoscope, syringes, bandages, purse, shopping bags, pet carrier and tools
- A set of cups and saucers, plates and cutlery with toy food such as bread, fruit, vegetables, biscuits
- A till with a range of plastic coins and notes
- A selection of costumes and props for fantasy play such as chiffon scarves, feather boa, tiara, wands
- One or two soft toy pets
- A range of equipment for writing such as notebooks, clipboards and chalkboards to make hanging signs etc

Resource Organisation

- Clothes hung up on hooks
- Props and artefacts organised into collections according to theme e.g. real-life accessories
- Resources stored in clearly labelled baskets

Experience Offered

- Plan and create real-life and imaginative settings such as shops, police station, medical centres, fictional settings
- Select the resources needed to establish the space and set them up according to the plan
- Introduce the setting to their peers, explaining the roles involved
- Use clothes and costumes to dress up as characters
- Play in character, using different voices and expressions, recreating and acting out familiar and imaginative scenarios; serving a customer, treating a patient
- Retell familiar stories and develop story themes and ideas, making alternative endings and changes to the setting/plot/characters
- Experiment with and embed a wide range of vocabulary associated with the roles they play

Vocabulary

English
Character, setting, first, next, then, last, after a while, finally, eventually, meanwhile

Maths
Before, after, next, first, today, yesterday, tomorrow, morning, afternoon and evening, o'clock, half past, quarter to/past, money, coin/note values, more than, less than, remaining

Recording Opportunities

- Plan the role play setting e.g. through listing the resources required when establishing a new context
- Create labels and signs for role-play settings
- Create forms and charts for use during play e.g. appointment cards, telephone messages, contact details, menus
- Writing during play such as taking orders, recording incidents, reports and record keeping

Enhancement Ideas

- Clothing and resources linked to characters in class books, themes or children's interests
- Resources to provoke further developments in play such as a clothing rail, a sale poster or an injured toy animal
- Images, posters and signs from a shop or a surgery, for example
- Resources added to other provision areas, such as the workshop to support the development of a role play context
- Books, film clips or visitors to support information gathering when planning and developing a role play context
- Visits to settings that are going to be developed in the classroom

Engage with **@earlyexcellence** on our social media channels & visit
earlyexcellence.com/subscribe to receive the latest updates

© Early Excellence Ltd 2021

55

Enquiry Area

XƎ Early Excellence
Inspirational Learning

Learning Intentions Y1/Y2/KS1 National Curriculum

English

- Listen and respond appropriately to adults and their peers
- Ask relevant questions to extend their understanding and knowledge
- Articulate and justify answers, arguments and opinions
- Give well-structured descriptions, explanations and narratives for different purposes
- Maintain attention and participate actively in collaborative conversations, staying on topic and initiating and responding to comments
- Use spoken language to develop understanding through speculating, hypothesising, imagining and exploring ideas
- Gain, maintain and monitor the interest of the listener(s)
- Consider and evaluate different viewpoints, attending to and building on the contributions of others
- Develop pleasure in reading, motivation to read, vocabulary and understanding
- Apply their growing phonic knowledge and skills to decode words
- Develop pleasure in reading, motivation to read, vocabulary and understanding
- *Work with non-fiction books that are structured in different ways*
- Discuss and clarify word meanings, linking new meanings to those already known
- Explain and discuss their understanding of books
- *Write sentences by saying out loud what they are going to write about*
- Re-read what they have written to check that it makes sense
- Discuss what they have written with the teacher or other pupils
- Write down ideas and/or key words, including new vocabulary
- Write for a range of purposes, using taught concepts
- Apply simple spelling rules and guidance, as listed in English Appendices 1&2

Maths

- Recognise and use language relating to dates, including days of the week, weeks, months and years
- *Choose and use appropriate standard units to estimate and measure temperature (°C) using thermometers*

Computing

- Use technology purposefully to create, organise, store, manipulate and retrieve digital content

Learning Behaviours

Dispositions & Attitudes

- Making decisions about the resources they need
- Carefully observing, noticing and investigating resources, sharing and talking about what they notice
- Asking questions and making decisions about how they might best be answered
- Sharing and explaining their ideas and research with others
- Cooperating with their peer and sharing resources
- Testing ideas and theories
- Developing ways of recording and documenting their experiences and ideas
- Experimenting with and using an increasing range of vocabulary to formulate and describe their ideas and hypotheses

Science

- Ask simple questions and recognise that they can be answered in different ways
- Observe closely, using simple equipment
- Perform simple tests
- Identify and classify
- Use their observations and ideas to suggest answers to questions
- Gather and record data to help in answering questions
- Identify and name a variety of common plants and animals including fish, amphibians, reptiles, birds and mammals that are carnivores, herbivores and omnivores
- Identify and describe the basic structure of a variety of common flowering plants, including trees
- Compare and group together a variety of everyday materials on the basis of their simple physical properties.
- Observe changes across the four seasons
- Observe and describe weather associated with the seasons and how day length varies
- *Explore and compare the differences between things that are living, dead, and things that have never been alive*
- *Identify and name a variety of plants and animals in their habitats, including microhabitats*

Geography

- Name and locate the world's seven continents and five oceans
- Name, locate and identify characteristics of the four countries and capital cities of the United Kingdom and its surrounding seas
- Identify seasonal and daily weather patterns in the United Kingdom and the location of hot and cold areas of the world in relation to the Equator and the North and South Poles
- Use world maps, atlases and globes to identify the United Kingdom and its countries, as well as the countries, continents and oceans studied at this key stage
- Use simple compass directions (North, South, East and West) and locational and directional language [for example, near and far; left and right], to describe the location of features and routes on a map
- Use aerial photographs and plan perspectives to recognise landmarks and basic human and physical features

History

- Explore changes and events within living memory and the lives of significant individuals from the past
- Learn about significant historical events, people and places in their own locality

– Learning objectives introduced in yr2

KS1 Practice & Provision / Teaching & Learning

Key Resources

Science

- Simple globe, world map and atlas
- Maps of the local area and places with which the children are familiar
- Aerial photographs of the local area including the school grounds
- Images of key features and buildings in the local area and further afield such as castles, shopping centres, beaches, rivers
- Magnifying glasses and collection pots
- A compass and pairs of binoculars
- Sorting trays and resources to group, classify and display objects such as wooden rings or cutlery trays
- Measurement equipment and mathematical recording resources such as tally and bar chart formats
- Equipment and recording resources to monitor the weather including an outdoor thermometer and wind gauge
- A selection of writing/drawing resources to support the making of labels, signs and diagrams including observation journals, parcel labels and card holders
- A set of mirrors and magnets
- IT equipment including laptops/ipad and camera (or made available when required)
- A small selection of key non-fiction texts and identification charts for frequent reference e.g. to identify birds and trees in the local area
- Non-fiction books, images and artefacts linked to current teaching theme or children's interests

Resource Organisation

- An area with table(s) and chairs, and open shelving to display books and artefacts
- An additional space such as a low table or light box, to display a provocation, enhancement or objects the children may find
- Groups of small resources organised into boxes or baskets
- Individual artefacts displayed attractively, using stands or clear display boxes
- Space for children to explore the resources, work with reference books and record their ideas and findings
- Area for children to display their collections

Experience Offered

- Observe closely, draw and ask questions about artefacts
- Use equipment and tools such as quadrats or charts to collect and record information
- Sort and classify artefacts and information
- Ask questions and make suggestions about what they observe or find out
- Make comparisons between objects and materials
- Carry out simple tests
- Use measurements in a range of contexts
- Use non-fiction books and IT (with appropriate levels of support) to find out about something that interests them or a current area of learning, following lines of enquiry
- Use identification books/charts to further their knowledge and vocabulary
- Identify places, features and routes on maps or aerial photographs
- Follow a cycle of enquiry as they question, research and finally present their findings

Vocabulary

Science
Scientist, scientifically, question, find out, research, observe, describe, test, compare, record, measure, information, fact

Computing
Content, organise, store, save, web, search, share

Recording Opportunities

- Record questions, ideas and thoughts in response to images, information or artefacts
- Make careful, labelled diagrams and observational drawings
- Record measurements
- Gather and record data, test results
- Create fact sheets, written accounts and non-fiction texts to share information with others
- Plan and evaluate practical work

Enhancement Ideas

- Fiction and non-fiction books that focus on children's interests or current themes
- Photographs or diagrams of structures made using the resources provided, including some by other children
- Instruction leaflets for the resources provided, as well as other structures, such as flat-pack furniture
- Photographs of structures such as truss bridges, vehicles, and sculptures
- Close up images and/or diagrams of engineering details such as struts, roof joists or axels
- Small scale models or artefacts that demonstrate key principles such as clock or machine parts, moving toys

Engage with **@earlyexcellence** on our social media channels & visit
earlyexcellence.com/subscribe to receive the latest updates

© Early Excellence Ltd 2021

57

Water Area

Early Excellence
Inspirational Learning

Learning Intentions Y1/Y2/KS1 National Curriculum

English

– Listen and respond appropriately to adults and their peers
– Ask relevant questions to extend their understanding and knowledge
– Give well-structured descriptions, explanations and narratives for different purposes, including for expressing feelings
– Use spoken language to develop understanding through speculating, hypothesising, imagining and exploring ideas

Maths

– Compare, describe and solve practical problems for capacity and volume [for example, full/empty, more than, less than, half, half full, quarter]
– Measure and begin to record capacity and volume
– *Choose and use appropriate standard units to estimate and measure capacity (litres/ml) to the nearest appropriate unit, using measuring vessels*
– *Compare and order volume/capacity and record the results using >, < and =*

Science

– Ask simple questions and recognising that they can be answered in different ways
– Observe closely, using simple equipment
– Perform simple tests
– Use their observations and ideas to suggest answers to questions
– Describe the simple physical properties of a variety of everyday materials

Design & Technology

– Generate, develop, model and communicate their ideas
– Explore and use mechanisms in their products

Learning Behaviours

Dispositions & Attitudes

– Making decisions about the resources they need
– Planning and communicating their ideas
– Expressing their thoughts and ideas to others
– Co-operating with peers, sharing resources and developing ideas together through planning, helping, negotiating and compromising
– Adapting and modifying their ideas, using trial and error
– Reflecting on and discussing the progress and outcome of their ideas
– Persisting with an idea through to a conclusion

– Learning objectives introduced in yr2

KS1 Practice & Provision / Teaching & Learning

Key Resources

- Collection of clear, graded cylinders, jugs and bottles incorporating scales
- Set of clear funnels
- Pipettes, syringes and basters of different capacities and lengths of clear tubing
- A set of connecting pipes
- A selection of natural resources such as wood slices, wood and bamboo lengths, natural sponge and shells
- A variety of cork pieces and shapes
- Small world fish, sea creatures, divers and pirates
- Wooden boats
- Child-sized mop and bucket

Resource Organisation

- Distinct area with non-slip wet flooring, ideally near a tap
- Transparent water tray or a selection of smaller bowls, according to the space available
- Larger items placed individually on shelves with labelled silhouettes to identify where they go
- Graded beakers, cylinders and jugs organised by height order
- Small resources grouped according to material or theme, displayed in plastic trays
- Text/numerals (with photographs if appropriate) used for labels

Experience Offered

- Developing fine motor skills through filling, emptying, joining and constructing
- Filling and measuring containers with increasing accuracy, comparing and ordering capacities, and reading scales
- Creating waterways by joining pipes and tubes
- Moving water at different rates and in different directions
- Describing the properties of water and its movement
- Investigating the behaviour of different materials in water including floating, sinking and how they can be moved
- Explaining their ideas, describing their actions and what they see happening
- Creating real and imagined settings and inventing narratives or events based on real-life scenarios

Vocabulary

English
Describe, explain, discuss, first, next, then, last, after that, finally, setting, character, plot, beginning, middle, end, event

Maths
Container, measure, capacity, compare, full/empty, more than, less than, half/quarter, scale, litre, millilitre, equal, same as, about the same as, more than, less than

Science
Equipment, measure, record, observe, compare, describe, explore, wood, bamboo, cork, plastic, metal, solid, bendy

Design & Technology
Plan, design, investigate, dismantle, join, connect, construct, structure, engineer, evaluate, instructions

Recording Opportunities

- Create mathematical statements referencing the capacity of containers etc, using symbols including +, -, >, < and =
- Draw labelled diagrams of their structures
- Write a series of instructions re how to use their moving water structure
- Create caption cards and labels for settings and narratives
- Photograph key points of narratives before developing into a small book/graphic story
- Take an aerial photograph of their setting then annotate or develop into a map
- Complete story maps based on their created narratives

Enhancement Ideas

- Containers of different depths, sizes and shapes to contain the water and for water to be moved between
- Resources to add scales to containers such as coloured tape and marker pens
- Images and diagrams of water in natural and man-made contexts such as waterfalls, dams or water wheels
- Videos or working models of structures that are moved by water
- Boats, rafts and other water toys that move using different mechanisms
- Materials to build and experiment with for example plasticine, foil pieces or trays, corks and cocktail sticks

Engage with **@earlyexcellence** on our social media channels & visit **earlyexcellence.com/subscribe** to receive the latest updates

© Early Excellence Ltd 2021

Sand Area

Early Excellence
Inspirational Learning

Learning Intentions Y1/Y2/KS1 National Curriculum

English

- Listen and respond appropriately to adults and their peers
- Ask relevant questions to extend their understanding and knowledge
- Give well-structured descriptions, explanations and narratives for different purposes
- Use spoken language to develop understanding through speculating, hypothesising, imagining and exploring ideas

Maths

- Compare, describe and solve practical problems for capacity and volume [for example, full/empty, more than, less than, half, half full, quarter]
- Measure and begin to record capacity and volume
- *Choose and use appropriate standard units to estimate and measure capacity (litres/ml) to the nearest appropriate unit, using measuring vessels*
- *Compare and order volume/capacity and record the results using >, < and =*
- *Order and arrange combinations of mathematical objects in patterns and sequences*

Science

- Ask simple questions and recognise that they can be answered in different ways
- Observe closely, using simple equipment
- Perform simple tests
- Use their observations and ideas to suggest answers to questions
- Describe the simple physical properties of a variety of everyday materials

Design & Technology

- Generate, develop, model and communicate their ideas
- Explore and use mechanisms in their products

Learning Behaviours

Dispositions & Attitudes

- Making decisions around the resources they need
- Taking responsibility for the organisation of the area and care of resources
- Expressing their thoughts and ideas to other
- Cooperating effectively and sharing resources appropriately
- Using a growing range of interesting and appropriate vocabulary
- Expressing their ideas creatively

– Learning objectives introduced in yr2

KS1 Practice & Provision / Teaching & Learning

Key Resources

- Natural or coloured sand either in a large tray or stored in containers for children to select
- Spray bottle
- Set of graded jugs and beakers
- Set of small buckets and eggcups
- Selection of sand tools including rakes and finishing trowels, sieves and measuring spoons and potato masher
- Selection of spoons, spreaders and scoops of various sizes, and measuring spoons
- A collection of natural materials e.g. stones, pebbles, wooden logs & poles
- Small world sets of small world wild animals and dinosaurs (may be miniature)
- High quality texts or images , relating to current themes/interests
- Broom/dustpan & brush

Resource Organisation

- Tray or container(s) to fit the available space – can be done in miniature
- Open shelving/surface to store resources
- Larger resources stored directly on shelves, with labelled silhouettes identifying their place
- Graded beakers & jugs organised by height
- Collections of smaller resources grouped according to use and/or material, in plastic trays
- Text (with photographs if appropriate) used for labels

Experience Offered

- Developing fine motor skills through filling, emptying, manipulating, marking and shaping sand
- Filling and measuring containers with increasing accuracy, comparing and ordering capacities, and reading scales
- Creating shapes, patterns and designs with resources and by marking & shaping the sand
- Noticing and comparing the texture and properties of dry, damp & wet sand
- Explaining their ideas, describing their actions and what they see happening
- Creating real and imagined settings and inventing narratives or events based on real-life scenarios

Vocabulary

English
Describe, explain, discuss, first, next, then, last, after that, finally, setting, character, plot, beginning, middle, end, event

Maths
Container, measure, capacity, compare, full/empty, more than, less than, half/quarter, scale, litre, millilitre, pattern, symmetrical, sequence, order, 3D, 2D

Science
Equipment, measure, record, observe, compare, describe, similar/ similarity, different/differences, explore, wood, bamboo, plastic, metal, solid, bendy

Art & Design
Create, design, texture, line, pattern, form, shape, space, mould

Recording Opportunities

- Create mathematical statements referencing the capacity of containers etc, using symbols including +, -, >, < and =
- Create caption cards and labels for settings and narratives
- Photograph key points of narratives before developing into a small book/graphic story
- Take an aerial photograph of their setting then annotate or develop into a map
- Complete story maps based on their created narratives

Enhancement Ideas

- A selection of trays and containers of different shapes and sizes, to hold the sand
- Resources that can be used to shape or mould the sand in different ways
- Natural resources to create patterns and designs
- Tools and resources that can be used to create marks and patterns in damp sand
- Books and images of structures made in sand or set in sandy locations such as deserts of beaches
- Small world creatures or construction vehicles

© Early Excellence Ltd 2021

Engage with **@earlyexcellence** on our social media channels & visit
earlyexcellence.com/subscribe to receive the latest updates

Art Area

Learning Intentions Y1/Y2/KS1 National Curriculum

Art & Design

- Use a range of materials creatively to design and make products
- Use drawing, painting and sculpture to develop and share their ideas, experiences and imagination
- Develop a wide range of art and design techniques using colour, pattern, texture, line, shape, form and space
- Learn about the work of a range of artists, craft makers and designers, describing the differences and similarities between different practices and disciplines, and making links to their own work.

Design & Technology

- Generate, develop, model and communicate their ideas through talking and drawing
- Select from and use a range of tools and equipment to perform practical tasks (for example, cutting, shaping, joining and finishing)
- Select from and use a wide range of materials and components, including textiles according to their characteristics

English

- Listen and respond appropriately to adults and their peers
- Ask relevant questions to extend their understanding and knowledge
- Articulate and justify answers, arguments and opinions
- Give well-structured descriptions, explanations and narratives for different purposes, including for expressing opinions

Learning Behaviours

Dispositions & Attitudes

- Making decisions about the subject and/or resources they are going to use
- Exploring and experimenting with tools, media and techniques
- Expressing their ideas creatively
- Incorporate an increasing range of skills and techniques in their work, making links between taught concepts and their own ideas
- Responding with imagination to provocations
- Evaluating and reflecting on their work and that of their peers
- Choosing what to display and how to display it, creating signs and captions to inform others

History

- Learn about the lives of significant individuals in the past who have contributed to national and international achievements

– Learning objectives introduced in yr2

KS1 Practice & Provision / Teaching & Learning

Key Resources

- Choice of paper and card in a range of colours and textures, that can be cut to the desired shape and size
- A selection of paint brushes of different sizes and lengths including flat, round and pointed tips
- Sketching and drawing pencils of different grades e.g. 2B, 4B, coloured pencils, oil pastels, chalk and charcoal
- Additional paint tools such as sponges, scrapers, painting knives and stencils
- Printing tools such as textured rollers and printing blocks
- Water pots, paint trays, paint pots, flat and divided palettes
- Clay boards and tools
- Ready mixed or powder paint in primary colours, black and white with resources for mixing e.g. containers, scoops, spoons, pipettes or syringes
- Block paints and watercolour sets
- Clay or resources to make salt dough
- Clipboards to support painting/drawing outside of the painting area
- Resources which can be added to paint which support exploration of texture such as glue, salt or sand
- Resources for labelling/signage of work when displayed
- Images or books displaying art work of various styles or themes including artists and crafts people at work

Vocabulary

Colour, line, shape, texture, primary, secondary, mix, light, dark line, thick, thin, soft, broad, narrow, fine, straight, wavy, smooth, warm, cool, tone, tint, shade, shadow, dull, bright, pattern, 3D, 2D, sketch, drawing, sculpture, statue, model, painting, print, rubbing, collage, design, textile, observation, materials, foreground, background, portrait, landscape, shape, detail, charcoal, coloured, pencil, drawing pencil, watercolours, powder paint, clay, thread, weave

Resource Organisation

- Area located in a space with good natural light, if possible, placed close to the workshop area and sink
- An easel, if available, and one or two tables, where children can sit or stand when working
- Resources organised on open shelving or a mobile trolley, stored in trays that are easily accessed by the children
- Paper and card organised in shallow trays or directly on shelves, rolls of paper on stand/wall
- Resources silhouetted where appropriate and clearly labelled
- A drying rack(s) for completed pieces and work-in progress
- An area to display provocations e.g. in a display cube, on a display stand or lit by a lamp
- A gallery area for children to display their art work, both 2D and 3D

Recording Opportunities

- Draw/write their plans or ideas e.g. listing what they might use or collecting ideas and inspiration
- Make notes in a sketchbook, for example, about approaches they have taken or when evaluating their work
- Write titles, captions and descriptions of their art for gallery display labels

Experience Offered

- Produce creative work in 2D and 3D working with a wide range of media
- Use drawing, painting, sculpture and other art, craft and design techniques to explore their own ideas and in response to their own experiences
- Experiment with the approaches of artists and craft makers, reproducing and combining techniques and materials in their own pieces
- Paint/decorate models that they have made in other areas of provision e.g. workshop, adding details and design features
- Create resources to support learning in other subjects
- Follow instructions to perform particular techniques or prepare resources

Enhancement Ideas

- Books and images that focus on the work of other artists
- Images of art and craftwork focussed on a particular theme e.g. trees or people
- Tools to support focussed investigations such as palette knives
- Artefacts such as natural resources or machine parts to support observational artwork
- Images or film links of artists/craftspeople at work, or visitors
- Sets of instructions for how to draw a range of objects

Engage with @earlyexcellence on our social media channels & visit
earlyexcellence.com/subscribe to receive the latest updates

Workshop Area

XE Early Excellence
Inspirational Learning

Learning Intentions Y1/Y2/KS1 National Curriculum

English

– Listen and respond appropriately to adults and their peers
– Ask relevant questions to extend their understanding and knowledge
– *Write down ideas and/or key words, including new vocabulary*
– Write sentences, captions and labels using taught concepts and structures
– Re-read what they have written to check that it makes sense, *proofreading to check for errors*

Maths

– Read and write numbers from 1 to 20 in numerals and words *and to at least 100 in numerals and in words*
– Compare, describe and solve practical problems for lengths and heights [for example, long/short, longer/shorter, tall/short, double/half]
– Measure and begin to record lengths and heights
– *Choose and use appropriate standard units to estimate and measure length/height*
– Recognise and name common 2D and 3D shapes, *identify and describe their properties*
– *Identify 2D shapes on the surface of 3D shapes*

Science

– Distinguish between an object and the material from which it is made
– Identify and name a variety of everyday materials, including wood, plastic, glass, metal, water, and rock
– Describe the simple physical properties of a variety of everyday materials
– Compare and group together a variety of everyday materials on the basis of their simple physical properties
– *Identify and compare the suitability of a variety of everyday materials, including wood, metal, plastic, glass, brick, rock, paper and cardboard for particular uses*
– *Find out how the shapes of solid objects made from some materials can be changed by squashing, bending, twisting and stretching*

Art & Design

– Use a range of materials creatively to design and make products
– Use drawing, painting and sculpture to develop and share their ideas, experiences and imagination
– Develop a wide range of art and design techniques in using colour, pattern, texture, line, shape, form and space
– Learn about the work of a range of artists, craft makers and designers, describing the differences and similarities between different practices and disciplines, and making links to their own work

Design & Technology

– Design purposeful, functional, appealing products for themselves and other users based on design criteria
– Generate, develop, model and communicate their ideas through talking, drawing, templates and mock-ups
– Select from and use a range of tools and equipment to perform practical tasks [for example, cutting, shaping, jo ning and finishing]
– Select from and use a wide range of materials and components, including textiles, according to their characteristics
– Explore and evaluate a range of existing products
– Evaluate their ideas and products against design criteria
– Build structures, exploring how they can be made stronger, stiffer and more stable
– Explore and use mechanisms [for example, levers, sliders, wheels and axles], in their products

Learning Behaviours

Dispositions & Attitudes

– Making decisions about the resources they need
– Planning and communicating their ideas
– Expressing their thoughts and ideas to others
– Co-operating with peers and sharing resources
– Handling equipment safely and caring for resources
– Talking about what they are doing, describing their actions, what they see happening, sharing their ideas
– Making choices, finding solutions, using trial and error
– Adapting and modifying ideas, using trial and error
– Reflecting on progress and the outcome of their idea
– Picking those that are most suitable for their needs
– Experimenting with and using a range of vocabulary to describe their designs and ideas

– Learning objectives introduced in yr2

KS1 Practice & Provision / Teaching & Learning

Key Resources

- A selection of model making materials of different sizes and materials including cardboard boxes, cereal boxes, tubes, paper, card
- A selection of collage and decorative materials such as fabrics pieces, ribbon, buttons and lolly sticks
- A selection of fixing resources and ties including masking tape, duct tape, treasury tags, paper fasteners, elastic bands, staplers, wool, string, pipe cleaners, glue sticks and PVA
- A selection of tools for cutting, joining and measuring, including scissors, hole punch, tape measures, rulers and spirit levels
- A range of mark making equipment of different types and colours

Resource Organisation

- Area located close to art area
- A large table or worktop, ideally one that children can stand at
- Space for work in progress and a gallery to display finished pieces
- Open-ended shelving to store resources
- Collections of making resources grouped according to material and displayed in small, plastic boxes
- Tools and resources for joining grouped together in small boxes
- Resources labelled according to materials and/or their properties

Experience Offered

- Developing hand eye coordination and dexterity
- Using fine motor skills with increasing accuracy through manipulating, cutting and joining, in increasingly sophisticated way
- Opportunities to practise joining techniques
- Creating mock-ups before final pieces are started
- Adding details to models using different decorative techniques
- Exploring the properties of materials and making a selection accordingly, in relation to their chosen purpose

Vocabulary

English
Describe, explain, discuss, first, next, then, last, after that, finally, setting, character, plot, beginning, middle, end, event

Science
Wood, plastic, glass, metal, water, rock, brick, stone, foil, cotton, paper, fabric, textile, elastic, ribbon, etc hard/soft, stretchy/stiff, shiny/dull, rough/smooth, bendy/not bendy, waterproof/not waterproof, absorbent/not absorbent, opaque/transparent, natural, man-made, recycled

Design & Technology
Plan, design, purpose, model, product, structure, finish, materials, tool, build, join, attach, names of key equipment used, join, connect, construct, structure, mechanism, hinge, slider, lever, pivot, axle, flap, flange, buttress, tab, insert, slot, L-brace, engineer, architect, evaluate, instructions

Maths
Measure, long/short, longer/shorter, tall/short, double/half, compare, centimetre/cm, estimate, 2D/3D shapes, face, edge, side

Art & Design
Texture, shape, sculpture, construct, collage, finish, artist, sculptor, craft maker, designer

Recording Opportunities

- Produce labelled diagrams of their products/models/sculptures
- Finding other ways to record ideas
- Drawing their models with increasing accuracy, using straight lines and measurements e.g. to actual size or 1:2 scale
- Labelling design elements or measurements prior to photographing
- Create instructions for their products that others can follow, using images and/or text
- Create labels, captions and signs for their displayed models

Enhancement Ideas

- Examples of models and structures made by other people, including their peers
- Images or films of models being created, for example puppets or masks
- Books, photographs and images relating to current themes or interests
- Different or unusual making resources, such as packaging materials or the broken parts of object or toys
- Tools to create particular effects such as shaped craft punches or pattern cutting scissors
- Instructions for making cardboard models or moving mechanisms

© Early Excellence Ltd 2021

Engage with @earlyexcellence on our social media channels & visit
earlyexcellence.com/subscribe to receive the latest updates

Early Excellence
Inspirational Learning

Learning Behaviours

Learning Intentions Y1/Y2/KS1 National Curriculum

KS1 Practice & Provision / Teaching & Learning

Key Resources	Resource Organisation	Experience Offered

Vocabulary	Recording Opportunities	Enhancement Ideas

Be Inspired & Stay Ahead of Best Practice

Access videos, blogs and podcasts to inspire your thinking

At Early Excellence, promoting best practice in Early Primary Education is our mission. Everything we do from our online and onsite training, bespoke consultancy and school improvement services; through to our learning walks, videos, podcasts and blogs - aims to inform and inspire your practice.

Staying connected with our work and becoming part of a rich learning community has never been easier. Simply subscribe to our emails and social media channels to receive regular updates and be the first to access our fantastic range of free resources and events. So, whether you need some inspiration to refresh your Early Years or Key Stage 1 practice or are looking for expert support to help you develop a long term improvement strategy; our highly experienced team of Curriculum Consultants are here to support you.

Shop for specialist resources and books in our centre or online

Sign-up Today

To connect with our work and gain access to advice and support for EYFS & KS1 go online:
earlyexcellence.com/subscribe

Be Inspired & Stay Ahead of Best Practice

Join online events and meet our expert team

Explore onsite training for you and your team

Gain Help to Design Your Classrooms with Early Excellence

For help to design and equip your learning environments, simply contact Early Excellence. Our Curriculum Consultants are highly experienced at planning classrooms and will be happy to work with you to discuss your vision, plan your space and produce classroom designs for you to share and approve.

We specialise in fully resourcing classrooms and offer complete, readymade collections for all aspects of provision, each carefully curated for continuity of access and progression of learning from 2 to 7yrs.

With each classroom design comes a detailed list of all the resources you need to establish a rich and stimulating environment - and through our in-house delivery team we are able to offer you a personalised, well-managed delivery service to help make setting up your classrooms easy.

Access consultant-led expertise to design your classrooms

Contact Early Excellence for Support & Advice

Enquire about our FREE planning service and gain help to design your classrooms.

Contact Early Excellence on:
01422 311 314
admin@earlyexcellence.com

Gain detailed plans to help you maximise the use of your space

A bird's eye view. Digital plans of your classroom for you to share

Work with our team to choose and order all of your resources

Learning transformed. A brand new classroom fully resourced for you

This will work well here! Discussing the layout of the classroom

Sit back and relax! Your order will be expertly managed & delivered by our highly experienced in-house delivery team

Contact Us

Get Connected

Visit
Early Excellence
The Old School, New Hey Road,
Outlane, Huddersfield HD3 3YJ.

Twitter
@earlyexcellence
Follow us and be the first to find
out about our announcements.

Telephone
01422 311 314
Call our team – we will be
pleased to help.

Facebook
facebook.com/earlyexcellence
Like us and share information
about our latest news and events.

Fax
01422 311 315
Send us a fax and we will come
back to you.

Pinterest
pinterest.com/earlyexcellence
Follow our board for visual
inspiration and new ideas.

Email
admin@earlyexcellence.com
Contact our team and we will
respond to your enquiry.

Instagram
instagram.com/earlyexcellence
Follow our page for images,
videos and conversation.

Online
www.earlyexcellence.com
Visit us to access all of our
services and find out more.

Linkedin
linkedin.com/in/early-excellence
-894419140/
Connect and keep updated.

Further Info

To enquire about Key Stage 1
equipment, contact us on
01422 311 314 or email
sales@earlyexcellence.com